# The Weirdest Things That Have Ever Happened to Me

Veronica Vulpine

authorHOUSE®

AuthorHouse™
1663 Liberty Drive
Bloomington, IN 47403
www.authorhouse.com
Phone: 1 (800) 839-8640

Published by AuthorHouse 10/25/2017

ISBN: 978-1-5462-1458-8 (sc)
ISBN: 978-1-5462-1457-1 (e)

Print information available on the last page.

This book is printed on acid-free paper.

I'm sure that everyone in life has that one pivotal moment, when they actually wonder if everyone's life is as shitty as theirs. Well, I'm here to tell you, that they are. My stepdad (my dad) always had a saying over the years that managed to stick with me forever, "Everyone is miserable in life, the only people you will ever be jealous of, are the ones that are just really good fucking liars." No truer words have been spoken! This novella is here to cheer you up!

# Weird Shit Involving Chocolate Animals

When I was a little, I was always brought up to be completely compassionate toward animals. This made me slightly weird, because every year when I would get my Easter basket, I would only eat the animal's chocolate bodies, but NEVER THEIR HEADS! So eventually I would end up every year with a basket full of heads! My parents would scream, "What the hell is it with this basket of heads?!?" "I don't want to hurt the animals!" I would scream back! What kind of reverse psychology was this? Love animals, don't eat them! I will still to this day never eat a chocolate bunny's head!

# Weird Shit Involving Real Animals

Anyway, I have never lived in the country before, but I am pretty well adept with dealing with anything...until somehow one night, this GIANT GREEN BAT GETS INTO MY HOUSE! This thing is stuck in the kitchen, flaying about and knocking shit over! Help, HELP! WE'LL ALL BE KILLED! CRASH! There goes another martini glass! Now, if you ever had good parents, they would have taught you the Golden Rule. If you completely hide under the covers, monsters CANNOT get you! I'm in my early twenties, and am now cowering under my comforter upstairs (which at this given time, WAS NOT VERY FUCKING COMFORTING!) SMASH! From downstairs! JESUS CHRIST! WHAT THE HELL WAS GOING ON DOWN THERE?!? A bar fight involving a lot of whiskey and PCP?!? I couldn't have made a tighter cocoon for myself! I could barely breathe! But at least I was safe from the uninvited intruder!

In the morning, things had a different perspective. I found the perpetrator. It wasn't a bat! After research, I found out it was a Luna Moth! (Which from the amount of dishes being thrown in my kitchen, furniture being knocked over, and assorted nick knacks being destroyed, I more or less referred to it as the Lunatic Moth!) If you are unfamiliar with these beautiful creatures, they are completely harmless, absolutely stunning, but are as big as both of your hands put together in some kind of fake butterfly shape! I find this engine of destruction, scoop it up with an envelope, and set him outside, probably sending him off to terrorize more home owners!

Anyway, when I worked for the Postal System, the one ABSOLUTE rule was that NOBODY EVER leaves their vehicle running or unattended! It was considered a federal offense, because someone could run off with the mail! Because everyone is breaking their necks to steal everyone else's unpaid bill statements! (I hear there is a huge demand for these!) Which is why when I stopped for the travesty on a dead end road out in the middle of nowhere, this in retrospect, was a terrible idea!

There is a brand new SUV parked in the snow with a man screaming and a lady, who was dressed to the nine's in a long, expensive leather coat with her hair perfectly coiffed, was running through the woods in a pair of Italian boots! Thinking that these nitwits from Jersey had just bumped a deer with their car and had no capabilities of mentally dealing with any such dilemmas, against my better judgment, I pull over to try and assist them. Then the epic disaster started. Happy domestic dispute! Apparently, the wife was an extreme cat lover, and HER HUSBAND WAS NOT! "There's two kittens in the woods!" she wailed! Her husband, completely berserk by this time screams, "We already have SEVEN FUCKING CATS, YOU FUCKING DUMB CUNT!

I simultaneously made two decisions here. Either A.) I leave, and let this hurricane of emotional destruction blow over, in the hopes that no one else but the cats end up in the woods besides the wife 6 feet under, or B.) I try and help this poor woman who, despite her best efforts to look spectacular to whatever place they were headed to, was completely in disarray, covered in tears and mascara everywhere! Dear, God, WHY?!? WHY CAN'T I JUST HAVE ONE FUCKING NORMAL DAY?!? So, I decide to help her. I go running through the woods and managed to tackle these two, little puffballs (it probably helped that I was wasn't wearing 5" Italian stilettos).

Well, I managed to catch them. Now I have one in each hand, like the most furriest Carnivorous Kitten Mittens that you can imagine! These two little bastards WOULD NOT STOP BITING ME! Now I'm screaming at the wife! WHAT THE FUCK AM I SUPPOSED TO DO WITH THESE?!? She's still hysterical, her husband is still shrieking, AND THESE THINGS ARE STILL ATTACHED TO MY HANDS AND ARE PSYCHOTIC!

She finally gets herself under control and asks if I would take them home, so her husband would not murder her. I tell her, NO, because my husband HATE'S cats, he would probably murder me AND ALSO THE CATS! Now she turns on the waterworks again. Oh, Jesus, why?!? So she makes a deal with me. If she sends me a check to get these things fixed, could I just keep them? At this point in time, between the repercussions of Federal prison for illegally stopping, and trying to end this crisis, I wave the white flag of surrender, and agree. The ravenous little beasts were ripped from me and unceremoniously thrown in my truck, and much like a horrific vehicle accident, numbers and addresses were exchanged. Off I go to finish my mail route with one bizarre twist! I could not find these tiny creatures of mayhem anywhere! Did they escape from the truck? Did I accidentally leave them attached to the mail in someone's mailbox? Were they in the backseat under packages, secretly plotting my demise? Where the hell were these little feline demons?!?

Now, I get home and tell my husband that I may have some bad news. He instantly says, "What, did you come home with some cats?" Most men would worry that a woman wrecked a car, mine was worried about cats! I say, "Well, I thought I brought a couple home, but I can't seem to find them. I think they are either in the fuse box or perhaps under the hood doing some transmission work." "Why do you have to be such a sarcastic ASSHOLE, Vaness?!?" was screamed! So we erected this giant parrot cage in the living room (which is weird that I owned one, because I've never even owned a parrot!) Bob goes out with a can of opened tuna, and these little hell spawn come flying out from under the seats to eat. Wanting to get them before they escaped, he grabs them in his giant paws of hands and takes them into the house to the cage. We fed them really well everyday with tuna, but these feral cats still had no interest in being friendly. Tons of endless hissing and growling! Morning, noon, and night! By now they are getting bigger. One day he goes to feed them, and the female latches onto his hand with the enragement of a wolverine with distemper! "Oh, my God! It's fucking got me!" he screams, while violently trying to disengage it! "Don't kill it!" I shriek! Total epic disaster was occurring! The cat was almost squished, and the cage was almost flipped over!

Finally, after a few weeks, the cats came to love us, though, and we let them out. Which was why I felt terrible when the check finally came in the mail. This lady was true to her word! Like the old adage, sometimes the check REALLY does come in the mail! So I take these animals to the vet to have them altered. All of my animals have always been fixed, but I felt terrible about keeping with this promise, because these two little indigents had finally trusted us! Well, The Gray Miser and Tiger managed to survive their reproductive removal ordeal, AND STILL LOVED US! My husband, who once vehemently hated cats as much as Ted Nugent, now loved these two! Especially the one that bit him! These cats still had the freedom to roam, because of the dog door on the back door, but they always rested inside.

Now, these weren't the only things smart enough to figure out how to use the dog door. For weeks, Bob kept telling me that there was a black cat living in our house. I thought he was screwing with me, until one day I am in the basement doing laundry and this thing comes out of nowhere hissing and growling up the staircase, AND SCARES THE SHIT OUT OF ME! I eventually made friends with it, but one day it just vanished, probably being some witches' familiar, and returning to his mistress of the dark realm. I tell this story to a guy at work, and he says the funniest thing. "What if you just thought that Bob had dementia, and had him put in an asylum, only to find out years later, that this thing really was living in stealth mode in your house like some invisible, subletting tenant?" Boy, either that would have caused a lot of problems, or solved a lot, in my opinion!

One day I am getting ready for work when it is still pitch black outside. My bathroom is directly next to the back door. I hear something trying with extreme diligence trying to get in. What could it be? The two cats were already indoors sleeping. Then, suddenly, this 45 pound raccoon comes bursting in. I'm not very well versed in the general temperament of these creatures, so I tried to emit the hospitality of Martha Stewart. "Welcome to Chez Vernoski. Would you care for any appetizers? Perhaps some anchovies with saltines?" No. This coon wanted nothing to do with me or my French food selection! He motored right by me to the kitchen, to the cat's Kit and Caboodle. Clearly, he was catering to his selective tastes!

Much like the black cat episode, how long had this been going on for?!? He seemed to know his way around the kitchen pretty well. I mean he wasn't at the stove with a "Kiss the Chef" apron on making Chicken Picante or anything, but he was well versed in his nightly routine. This has still been continuously going on for months! I wouldn't care, but for two reasons. I have to take my contacts out at night, and am pretty much legally blind without them. I would go downstairs at night to use the bathroom and TRIP OVER THIS THING! "Sorry, kitty!", I would say, thinking it was one of my cats. After falling over and bashing my head off of random kitchen appliances, telepathically, I could hear it shrieking back, "YOU STUPID, ASSHOLE, HUMAN! WHERE IS YOUR NOCTURNAL VISION?!?" Where was my vision in general? Where had it gone, really? (Had I stared at the sun too many times in grade school on dares?) Instead of biting me, this incredibly crafty bastard would high tail it out through the dog door.

This leads to the second reason that I wish it would stop visiting. It had no table manners! I would wake up in the middle of the night to its incessant crunching! I'm not sure what the noise was exactly. Was it redecorating the living room, running carpentry equipment, or JUST CHEWING WITH ITS MOUTH OPEN? That would be ultimately be followed by the sound of splashing in the cats' bowl. Was this thing running a Chinese laundry while I was trying to sleep?!? Perhaps reeling in a Marlin from deep sea fishing? Directing synchronized aquatic swimming classes? Running the dishwasher? WHAT?!?

Then one morning I get up and go downstairs without my contacts in, and see this giant brown blob sitting motionless on my kitchen floor. I go wandering back upstairs to regain my vision, and return back downstairs to find a Labrador still sitting motionless in the same spot, not even wagging its tail or blinking. Hi, Cujo! There were a ton of funny factors going on here. It was the neighbor's dog. I could tell by the tracker collar on it. Why he couldn't find it with that circuitry on was beyond me. Maybe my house was lead lined like a nuclear fallout shelter! In wondering if this dog was a statue, I reach down gingerly and poke its head. OH GOD PLEASE DO NOT BE A ZOMBIE DOG! I do not need a zombie dog in my house, because I only have one door inside, and it was for the bathroom behind it! But now it at least starts wagging its tail! OK, we were making progress!

Thinking that this poor mutt was starving, I start rooting through the fridge looking for anything to feed it. Unfortunately, my husband and I live like two bachelors, so there isn't any real food in there. I start feeding this poor thing anything I could find! A half eaten Italian hoagie, some potato salad, French fries, a container of yogurt, a pickled egg, and I think a container of horseradish shrimp dip! (Boy, was this poor thing's system going to be screwed up! God Bless his owner!)

Now, when my dogs would run away, they would escape over the mountain to my neighbor's house, and when his dogs would run away, they would run over the mountain to my house! Maybe if we just traded dogs, they would eventually end up at the right places! And how did this dog know how to use the back door? My neighbor always kept them in kennels. My cell phone for some inexplicable reason wouldn't work, so I couldn't even call him! And I was scared that if I tried to pick this thing up to put him in the dump truck, that he would get scared and bite me. (Also, I was scared that he would explode from the disgusting buffet that I had just fed him!) So I put a leash on him. "Come on, kiddo, let's go for a walk." The question here was who was walking who! After being dragged back to his owner's house unmercifully through extensive foliage, I finally put him back in one of the empty kennels. (Thankfully, the walk back was a lot less taxing!) This thoroughly confused the owner when he returned home after looking for him! How did the dog manage to escape and remanage to lock himself back in his pen?!? Was there some kind of teleportation powers and kinetic skills possessed by bird dogs?!? This had him baffled until later, when I called him from my husband's phone and explained. There went his ideas of a special breeding lineage! And probably for evading a shit storm of a kennel as well!

This brings me to the peacock. I have no idea what possesses me to do the things I do in life. I think it's a general mix between being bored with anything normal, and just plain old general alcoholism with heavy nicotine consumption on the side. Well, I just happened to find this bird for sale on Megslist two roads from my house! So I go and buy this poor thing from this crazed taxidermist. He tells me that he buys truckloads of these birds from Lancaster, and then stuffs them and sells them on the internet! The only reason he did not stuff this one in particular, is because it had really bad tail feathers, and it wasn't deemed financially viable. (Except he didn't say that, because I think that those multi syllable words were probably beyond the reaches of his vocabulary.) Anyway, this is learning lesson in life. Sometimes BEING A REJECT ACTUALLY SAVES YOUR LIFE! Don't be an overachiever! I love animals, and would have called PETA on this guy's ass, but he knew where I lived in the woods in the small town we're located in. The last thing I needed was to be stuffed with crossed eyes and bad sutures, being used for probably some sexual acts of abomination! So I had managed to save just one poor creature. It was the best I could do! I take this bird home in its canvas sack straight jacket, and put him in a 12' X 12' kennel. I realize this wasn't the Hotel Billton by any means, but it WAS a step up from being DEAD!

After a week, I feel bad about his incarceration, and having owned chickens before that had roamed about in the yard, I opened his door to total freedom! Well, this was a bad idea! Apparently, after months of emotional torture, he wanted even more freedom! So he takes off throughout the neighborhood, which is encompassed by a busy State Route! This bird, possessing an only pea sized brain, had managed to avoid being wailed by any fleet of triaxles, tanker trucks, or just drunken pickup drivers! So I start posting up fliers everywhere. "Have you seen this bird?" Now here was the weird part, after so many years of commuting to jobs, I had no idea WHO MY NEIGHBORS EVEN WERE! Now I knew everyone, because EVERYONE WAS CALLING ME! "Your bird is in my yard!" they would exclaim with delight! Now, this thing was slowly becoming a celebrity around town! Everyone knew it, and everyone loved it! People were taking pictures with it in their gardens, with their grandchildren next to it, on dirt roads, next to ponds, WHEREVER! Boy, can these things travel! We had tried pursuing catching it on many occasions, much to no avail! Let me tell you something about these birds. You may think that they are slow because of their shitty aerodynamics, but these little birds CAN MOVE!!! I don't care what a great track star you think you are, you are NEVER, EVER going to catch one of these! TRUST ME! And once they get a good running start, much like a little Piper Cub, they can launch themselves onto any tree branch available!

Finally, I gave up on trying to recall this poultry, which was when it returned home of its own account, my husband and I were completely rendered speechless. We were talking through the back doors of the house, when I spotted the iridescent blue out of the corner of my eye! "Don't make any sudden movements!" I whisper! "Go throw out some Kit and Caboodle!" This strange recipe of cat food managed to hypnotize this bird (much like other creatures) into not leaving the household. After months of chasing this little bastard around, he just returns like the prodigal child!

Strangely, this bird never left again, being satiated on cat food and PIZZA! That's right! This God Damned thing must have been of Italian heritage, because it wanted pizza! Not bread like pigeons, not grilled cheese, not Caprese Salad with Balsamic Reduction, IT JUST WANTED PIZZA! And it would get crabby if it didn't get it! Worried that it would once again cruise off, we placated it like Horus, the ancient, Egyptian deity! Would you like extra pepperoni on this tray, your Majesty? He apparently did! And he never left! Years later, he always still sleeps in the same tree, on the same tree branch, every night right next to my room!

Now, if you are unfamiliar with these creatures, they make great watch dogs! Any sounds or movement will drive them to epic shrieking! And they are loud! This particular bird had 3 settings. "HONK," "WAHH," and "BUT WHAT?" This is a great asset if you are a shadowy recluse like myself or are running a drug plantation and need prior warning to any invading authorities! The only problem was, ANYTHING WOKE THIS THING UP AT NIGHT! If I should turn on a light, open the refrigerator door for a midnight snack, or just try and use the bathroom, I would have to deal with his epic screaming for an hour! God Damn it bird, try some Ambien already! His favorite activity, though, would be to sit on the huge open trailer in the front yard and shriek at traffic all day! Also, he was extremely inquisitive, so everytime we would work on a project in the yard, he would come over and watch us. This is why he was deemed Construction Control Manger.

One day, two employees from the propane company were working on my tank in the yard. Well, this bugger sneaks up behind them, to see what they were doing. In the midst of their maintenance, he screams, "BUT WHAT?!?" and SCARES THE CRAP OUT OF THEM! "JESUS CHRIST!" they both yell in unison! And scatter! Apparently, the Construction Control Manager was unsatisfied at the job that they were doing! Good job at managing quality control around here, buddy!

Now, it gets very cold where I live in Eastern PA, and it snows a lot. And I would feel bad for this huge parrot of tropical descent. Our basement is unfinished, but warm because of the wood burner. So I would open the door, and in he would scoot! He would perch upon the bar on the weight bench (which was my excuse not to work out). We felt bad for him, so we gave him a big mirror and left a radio playing for him all day, while plying him with many assorted food offerings. But one year, he wouldn't come in! Thank God I happened to go outside, because this poor thing was stuck up in the woods in a snow drift! I'm only 5'4" and the snow we got was in three foot drifts! This rendered my efforts to reach him only to rival that of a Russian Icebreaker! I finally make it, and am faced with the harsh reality of, one screw up on my part, and this beautiful creature was going to escape, and probably freeze to death! So I launch myself at his tail and grab it. This was an absolute terrible decision! Mistakenly thinking that I was a predator, this thing puts up a fight of any renowned gladiator! If you've ever been hit in the face with a goose wing, IT FUCKING HURTS! I managed to relaunch myself completely on top of him to pin down his wings, which, in turn, lead to an alligator death roll through the woods, and almost over the embankment! Crisis situation overload! I am stuck in three feet of snow, on my back, with this huge bird pinned to my chest, AND I CAN'T GET UP BECAUSE I CAN'T USE MY ARMS AND HAVE NO LEVERAGE! "I HOPE YOU'RE HAPPY WITH YOURSELF, YOU ASSHOLE!" I indignantly scream! Then, strangely after all the physical exertion and all the adrenaline was out of our systems, I think we both inexplicably took a nap for ten minutes!

When I awoke, a wonderful idea, much like an epiphany, occurred to me! Ask God for help! So I said this prayer, "Dear God, I know I am a complete and total Pagan, and don't believe in you, but please don't let this beautiful animal die because of my stupidity. Amen." Now I hear the peacock screech in my head, "Why didn't you just let me die?!? I would've been happier then!" "SHUT UP," I scream! "NO ONE GETS TO BE HAPPY AROUND HERE!" And then I commenced pushing myself with my feet towards a tree, where I managed to upright myself, along with my precious cargo!

Then the unthinkable happened! While carting this gorgeous animal down the embankment, trudging through the waist deep snow, I accidentally stepped on its tail, which almost made me take a header over the embankment with it, probably causing us both to come to an untimely end! It was probably my errant prayer that saved us, because I caught myself in time! Now I am carrying this thing like a bride over the threshold into the house, and this poor thing was so resigned to its fate of indoor captivity, it totally stopped struggling (this may be because of partial thankfulness, or because of the fact of the delirium caused, when I probably crushed every vital organ in his fragile, petite body, when I fell on him.) So he goes wandering into the sun room, which he adamantly watched my husband clean the quarter mile driveway off through our huge picture windows. Now my husband comes in, and just as equally as frozen as the peacock and I, and says, "Wow, how did you manage to get Krayola in here?" Tired from my epic travesty, and not wanting to elaborate, I said, "I just opened the back door, and he waltzed right in!" The peacock, sensing my insincerity, was pissed off, and left the sunroom to go hopping down the basement steps to his usual winter time retreat. Thanks a lot, Big Bird!

This is another awesome story involving a bird. A sweet driver where I used to work, tells me that when he was a kid, he and the neighborhood kids used to have a pet crow!

Now, I love crows (sorry, corn farmers everywhere), because I know how smart they are. After years of commuting to work, and having almost hitting tons of stupid deer that would just randomly jump out in front of me, crows would actually be eating roadkill, and instead of flying away when seeing my car coming, they would just march over to the other side of the lines on the road, really pissed off, wait for my car to pass over their lunch box, and then march back over the lines again! (These birds, in my opinion, were actually more clever than most pedestrians or DOT workers! How did they know what the lines in the road frigging meant?!? They are just birds with the brain the size of some kind of protozoa!)

Anyways, all the children would take turns taking care of it! Now, this story was slightly illogical, because of several reasons. Crows are very intelligent, so I can't figure out how they ended up with one, unless it got boinked off of a car, or it fell out of its nest as a baby. Secondly, most boys are ill tempered, and I can imagine them shooting at them for fun with their BB guns. Thirdly, most boys are irresponsible, so the fact that this aviator didn't starve to death, was beyond me! But much like the peacock, it became a township celebrity! Every kid wanted to take turns carrying this thing around and nurture it! So, one weekend he gets visitation rights, and is SO EXCITED! He takes it home, and goes out to play Sunday morning before his mom makes dinner. Well, she always had the habit of relaxing on the back porch while it was cooking by having a smoke and a beer. (I think that this was super cool because, although it's considered the norm now, I'm pretty sure it was not acceptable in that era!) Anyway, this poor kid comes home to find the worst situation imaginable! The crow is on the picnic table, motionless, on its back, with its little feet stuck up in the air! "Mama, the crow is dead!" he shrieks! "The neighborhood kids are going to kill me!" His mother calmly says, "Honey, he's not dead, he's just drunk. I just gave him a little saucer of beer." I'm not really sure what parental skills were involved here, boredom or just trying to be hospitable to a guest, but his feathery friend was indeed shitfaced. And I'm also not sure what the recovery time is for such a lightweight, but he managed to survive this unintended bender. On to the next household!

This brings me to the two times I was almost mauled by turtles! FUCKING TURTLES!!! Who the fuck gets killed by a turtle?!? Well, one day, my husband and I were driving home from lunch at my father's house, when I see a HUGE turtle in the middle of the road! Not wanting it to get run over, I pull over, and try to save it. I go to pick this thing up, when my husband grabs me and starts shrieking, "Don't touch that, it's a snapper, AND IT WILL BITE ALL OF YOUR FINGERS OFF!" So he gets a stick and puts it close to it. Well, this creature, obviously of reptilian lineage involving rage disorder, launches itself forward, biting the stick into a 100 toothpick count! "That could've been your hand, you, idiot!" he screams! (Bob said that, not the turtle. But I sensed with a low level of telepathy, the turtle was also thinking that!) So then he gently goads it off the road.

The second time, I am working in a quarry, when a triaxle driver tells me that there is a turtle in the middle of our road.

(I should have learned my lesson earlier, but I am self aware of being a slow learner.) Once again, not wanting one to get run over, I go out with a shovel, scoop it up, and carry it over next to the retention pond, where I thought it would be safer and happier. Well, apparently, it was NOT VERY HAPPIER! I had interrupted its journey to where ever it was headed! Perhaps to see a mistress, to go to a carnival for funnel cakes, or to also travel with the proverbial chicken, that also crosses the road! Perhaps he and said chicken were hoping to jump a rail car somewhere like two vagabonds, in the dreams of viewing the American countryside! Well, now this thing is pissed, and starts chasing me up the embankment! Contrary to popular belief, of these things being slow, depending on their species, I am here to tell you THAT THEY ARE NOT! I'm still hauling ass up the hillside, trying to evade the scaly psychotic, while alternately trying to beat it away with the shovel! "I was only trying to help!" I scream! Thank God these things, possessed with supernatural speeds, have a low level of endurance for maintaining them! I finally make it to the safety of the road, when I shout, "Fuck, you, turtles everywhere! I hope all you subterranean wretches die!" God Damned, short legged bottom feeders!

# Other Things I Was Almost Mauled By

A poodle. I know you are thinking to yourself, "What the hell?" Now, I have owned many large dogs in life like Malamutes and German Shepherds, and I know that they probably have terrible reputations of being mean, but they are the most sweetest, docile creatures that you would ever want to meet. I have taken them on jobsites before, and never even needed a leash for them. All the employees loved them!

Well, one day I am jogging along the road when this lady accidentally leaves her front door open. That's when "Poodle Assault" occurred. These two things come running out after me! Now, I'm used to dealing with dogs before, so I knew enough to stop moving, drop my head, and hold my hand out, palm upward. This turned out to be a truly ineffective decision on my part, because the medium sized one managed to latch itself onto my left calf! And I am not talking a little nip here, I am talking "Full Blown Death Grip!" Where was my shovel now?!? What was worse, the turtles or the poodle?!? This is what I get for trying to be healthy! Probably rabies! I never sued because I love animals (probably more so than their owners sometimes.) I didn't want to see this mindless creature's head cut off if proper veterinarian papers could not be produced. Also, I was guilty of not having my own animals vaccinated, because everything where I live just gets eaten by coyotes anyway. So, really, what was the point? Happy peroxide showers!

# Weird Things Involving Other People With Disasters Caused by Alternate Forms of Wildlife

One day, I am running the scale house in the quarry that I worked at, when this driver comes up to the window to sign his paperwork. His left hand is terribly mutilated. Then he asks me if I want to know what happened to it. NO! I silently scream! I have always been raised to be polite, so I don't care if someone is missing an eye, a limb, or terribly disfigured, I will ABSOLUTELY NEVER ask questions! This would result in a swift and furious beating from my parents! So my first response was DEFINETLY NO!, but thinking that he burned it on his hot exhaust or even hotter engine block while trying to work on his truck, and just wanted to vent about the shitty aspects of the construction industry and vehicle maintenance, I agree. Then he proceeds to tell me the worst story ever! His wife and he were sleeping in bed one night, when he thinks he gets bitten by something. He smacks it off of him, and returns to his slumber. In the morning, he gets up to take a shower, AND HIS HAND IS KILLING HIM! So now he is under the water, WHEN ALL HIS

SKIN STARTS FALLING OFF OF HIM! He starts screaming to his wife to take him to the emergency room! This is where he found out that he had gotten bit by a Brown Recluse Spider! If, you are not familiar with these, they are very small, but VERY DEADLY!

Most people from this upper North Region worry about poisonous snakes like Copperheads or Rattlers, but you can easily spot one! But these little bastards, being both small, and thusly named Reclusive for their elusiveness, ARE MUCH WORSE! This only added for my hatred of spiders!

Now this poor couple have two, little kids. Terrified for their welfare, they come home, AND BURN EVERYTHING IN THE HOUSE LOOKING FOR THIS HELLACIOUS ARACHNID! THE MATRESSES, CURTAINS, FURNITURE, EVERYTHING! Then they have the whole house steam cleaned! AND STILL NO SPIDER TO BE FOUND ANYWHERE, ANYPLACE! I'm not sure what the life span of these things are, if it managed to produce any offspring, or if it had managed to pack its bags and head to some island cruise resort, but NOW THESE POOR PEOPLE WERE LIVING IN A MOTEL JUST TO ESCAPE THIS EIGHT LEGGED DEMON! OH, THE HORROR! Why couldn't a medieval dragon just have materialized to be dealt with?!?

Now I am terrified because I live in the country (did I also happen to mention how much I hate spiders?) and am scared shitless that one of these things were going to get me, too! So I started spending every night sleeping sitting up on the couch, with a blanket completely wrapped around me like an Indian Chief! This went on for weeks, until my hysteria died down! Sometimes in life, the unknown is worse than the bite!

# Weird Shit Involving Terrible Traffic Accidents

One night I am coming home from after work in the dark. I was driving my little Dodge Dakota pickup truck in the snow and had just left the liquor store. Now, I don't condone getting all twisted up and driving, but I think the DUI laws are a bit ridiculous. Everyone has a high tolerance for alcohol where I live, (although I do believe PA has the highest rate of alcoholism in the country.) Go coal cracker PA! So I am sipping on a bottle of Campari, driving on a back road, when the disaster occurred! A van was driving the opposite way, so I never saw the deer run around from behind it, until it was too late! I slammed on my breaks, but still managed to bump it. Everyone teases me that I drive like a snail, and I do! There was absolutely no damage to this little beast, so I am out there trying to revive it, much to no avail. (Trust me, this episode had nothing to do with the alcohol. It would have happened regardless.) So I call my friend that is a garage mechanic, crying, and tell him what happened. There is a dead deer, and my radiator is leaking antifreeze everywhere! "I can't drive this thing home!" I wail! "Don't worry," he says "I will call the town cop to come and get you!" "NO! I HAVE BEEN DRINKING!" I scream! "Well, are you utterly shitfaced?" he asks? "No, I'm fine but…" "I'm calling him right now, then!"

Oh, God, now utter paranoia sets in! I start flinging my $80.00 liquor order over the side of the guiderail, just before the cop shows up. He proclaims, "What a Shit Show!" And then proceeds to tell me to follow him to the mechanic's garage, and to shut my truck off if it overheats. We get there, and the mechanic exclaims, "I think we all need a little homemade wine to take the edge off!" And proceeds to pour all three of us a glass, himself, myself, and the cop that was on duty! Said cop says to me, "If you tell anyone about this, I swear to God, I will pistol whip you to death!" With which I replied, "Sir, I've really stopped giving a shit much about anything, whatsoever, after about 9 o'clock tonight!" Well, that pretty much sealed our friendship!

The next day, I am driving down Death Road with one of my friends looking for my booze. "Vaness, there are three miles of woods here, and it just snowed again last night! You are never going to find your stash!" he screams! But when there is alcohol about, I can locate it like a K9 drug team looking for heroin! "Stop right here!" I scream back. "Vaness, there is no way you can remember a tree!" I get out, and recover my order! "There is NO WAY you just did that!" he shrieks! I answered cryptically, "Sometimes, the forest just talks to me!" Off to imbibing at my house!

Now I am driving from the landfill one night in the wintertime. I used to have the bad habit of picking up a case of beer for the way home, but the kid that worked at the distributor was the most annoying human being ever! Once trapped inside with him in this place, he would never SHUT THE HELL UP! Me, being raised as a polite person, would be stuck listening to his stupid bullshit for a half hour before trying to escape! After a long day at work, this is the last thing I wanted to do! So this kid's annoyance actually saved my life! Not wanting to deal with his drivel, I didn't stop there that night. Driving home, SOBER, I go through Klark's Summit on RT 81, when I noticed how shiny the road was. If you're not from the North, and don't know what black ice is, IT WILL FUCKING KILL YOU! Driving through snow with four wheel drive, is fine, but BLACK ICE IS MOTHER NATURE'S WORST DESTRUCTION! So when I saw it, I knew enough NOT to hit the brakes! And to just let the truck coast…55…50…45…Then the disaster occurred! It turned sideways on me! I counter steered and it turned sideways again! Now it's sideways once again! AND YET ONCE AGAIN! This truck ends up skidding down over the median! It's a good thing that this thing ended up picking so much velocity up, because it probably would have flipped on me!

Have you ever had time slow down on you in such a horrific disaster, that you actually are pretty sure that you're in an alternate dimension? Suddenly, in a nanosecond, all kinds of thoughts start going through my head, strangely, but calmly! "What have I done with my life? If I die now, how clean is my house? WHY THE FUCK COULDN'T I HAVE PUT MY SEATBELT ON? IT WOULD'VE TAKEN ME THREE FUCKING SECONDS!!!" So now this truck has gained so much momentum, that I hit the bottom of the embankment, AND MANANGED TO COME SHOOTING UP THE OTHER SIDE INTO SOUTH BOUND TRAFFIC! I am perpendicular to on coming traffic, when I almost hit the guiderails! If a tractor trailer had been coming through at that particular time, I would have been dead! No one would be reading this right now! I get myself straightened out, and head home, where my shaking and puking continued for hours!

The next day at work, the quarry manager calls me. "Where the hell were you last night? Your front tires have grass in the rims, and they are both flat!!!" So, kindly he has a tire crew come in and put new ones on for me. Now here is the mystery that needs to be solved here. How did I manage to drive home and to work the next day only to have them go flat then? Tirestone, I need answers here! What the hell?!?

This brings me to the tale of my idiot brother. Everyone in this town is a total alcoholic. EVERYONE! But strangely, there are hardly any accidents! Somehow, living in this colder climate, our bodies have managed to process excessive amounts of alcohol to account for the freezing cold! (I think this works like putting additives in diesel vehicles in the winter so that they don't gel up.) Except for my brother! One night, he shows up laughing like a lunatic inside our house in the middle of the night, and wakes up my husband and I up! We always leave our doors unlocked, but, just like everyone else in town, we would always sleep with guns under our pillows! We both wake up screaming with pistols in our hands! My brother is still downstairs bellowing like a crazed loon! AAHHH! He's lucky he didn't get gut shot! But he was so intoxicated, I'm not even sure he would have even felt it! He is screaming that he wrecked his car! He blew through an intersection, and somehow managed to launch his car onto a stone wall! I am not condoning drinking and driving here, people, because I know innocent folks get accidentally killed or maimed by drunks all the time, with ironically said drunks usually leaving unscathed. But what I do hate with an unholy passion, are government workers, who are basically dumber than a box of hair! I throw him on the couch, and threaten his life if he dared to move! Then my husband and I go downtown to witness the carnage! His car was indeed tottering on a stone wall! My husband I both agreed that pulling this car off with our dump truck would manage to rip off the undercarriage. So we returned home to my house to visit my unconscious brother.

In the morning, I cart his stupid ass home. I drop him off at his house in his forlorn state, only to return home, and to have him call me and say that a state trooper was calling him about his car! (And everyone thinks that I am the family drunk! AT LEAST I AM A HIGHLY FUNCTIONING ONE!) So then I have to go back to pick him up to return to the scene of the crime. Well, he starts shrieking that he doesn't know what to say! (Way to go G-Boy! Try thinking for yourself when Big Brother isn't around doing it for you!) His car is wrecked, and the side of it is also wrecked from another earlier drunken accident.

Now, I am the world's most shittiest liar, but strangely, when terrified, I channel Sybil, and another Veronica takes over! Calmly I say, "Listen, this is what you are going to tell the trooper. You have been working swing shifts lately, were very tired, and just basically nodded off while driving. Then you tell him that the dent was already there when you originally bought the car. A guy at work wrecked it, needed money, and was selling it cheap because of that reason. And then tell him that you had no cell phone service there in which to call towing." Things were going great there with my previous prompting, until my brother's cell phone rang AND HE ANSWERS IT, RIGHT IN THE MIDDLE OF THE INTEROGATION! The statey and I both look at each other, and both face palm our heads! Keep working for the man, where thinking is optional! At least two of us had salvageable brains! Now I am forced to do the unthinkable! I knew the towing company that did all the hauling for the state police, and I was forced to throw its name down! "Don't worry, I have their personal number in my cell!" I proclaimed! "Really?" the trooper says! At this point in time, although I managed save my brother's general welfare with my connections, I felt like smashing his head in with a hammer!

I actually love state troopers. They are people that put up with so much shit, that I really don't know how they just don't murder irritating people or just drug hauling nut cases in general. Seriously, I once read that they and psychiatrists have the worst suicide rate. (Poor bastards. I mean the state police, not the people they have to deal with.) Town cops are actually mostly dicks, who got beat up in high school, and were looking to get back at the world! So one night when I, too, was coming home trashed, and saw the blueberries and cherries turn on in the parking lot, I immediately pulled over! I used to work with a concrete driver who would say, "I am an alcoholic, but that makes me a better driver, because I am so paranoid about being pulled over and losing my

CDL, that I pay more attention to my surroundings and environment than most people do!" This proclamation strangely, made odd sense to me!

The trooper comes over to my window, and asks why I thought that I was being stopped. Now, I used to work for this manager who had another great saying! "Vaness, when in doubt, throw the dumb bitch card out!" So simultaneously doing my best not to breathe on this guy and look adorable, I say "Um...no, sir." "Well, you were speeding, your front headlight is out, the glow lights on your hood are illegal, and I see that you are also not wearing your seat belt." Boy, that list was sure long! At least the fact that I was all twisted up wasn't included on it! I'm not sure if it was a shift change, or he just was tired, and didn't feel like doing any excess paperwork, but in the end, HE JUST ENDS UP LETTING ME GO! How much do I love these guys!?!

This is another story involving an awesome state trooper. When I worked at this one quarry down in Bethhateshim, they were so busy with production, that they would keep moving excavation into the woods. They would rip up beautiful Oak and Maple trees, and just bury them somewhere else! So then I get an idea (that is usually where trouble occurs on my part)! I had just bought a HUGE trailer and had a wood burner at home. This place was just basically just wasting these things, but I could use them! So I ask the quarry manager if I could cut them up and take them home. Strangely, liability issues aside, he says OK (I think it was because he was on a lot of psychoactive medication at the time). Then I ask my boss if I could use the loader after work to put these monstrous wooden beasts on my trailer, and strangely, he says OK, too! (I think it was because he just used to smoke a lot weed). "Just make sure the machine has enough fuel for the morning!", he says. Then I ask the excavator operator if he would be so kind as to start putting this hardwood in a pile for me. "Sure, Vaness, no problem", he says. (I think it was because he was just a raging alcoholic, like myself). Boy, were these people sure agreeable around there!

Even the state trooper that eventually pulled us over was agreeable! Now, here were the problems. It was a holiday weekend, and I should have known better, because, although, my husband chained this gigantic load down perfectly, it still stuck out like a logging truck! And although the truck and trailer were capable of handling this gigantic load, IT STILL STUCK OUT LIKE A FUCKING LOGGING TRUCK! And then, because I was working so many hours, I didn't have enough time to get a license plate on it! So I tell my husband to stay in front of me with the truck and trailer, and I would ride his bumper with my truck, so no police would notice that little discrepancy.

Well, this plan didn't happen according to my ill devised scheme! Heading home after a few exits, a trooper comes flying down off of the ramp, and somehow manages to get in between us without crashing! "Pull over, Bob!" I scream on the two-way! Then the inevitable happens! The blues and reds turn on! Oh, God, Almighty! We pull over, where I had the pleasure to meet the best trooper ever! He asks me why he pulled us over. That's where I had to throw down Mike Yuhaus's patented "Dumb Bitch Card!" "Um…I don't know, why?" I say. "WELL, YOU DON'T HAVE A LICENSE PLATE, THIS TRAILER ISN'T REGISTERED, AND IT LOOKS LIKE A GOD DAMN LOGGING TRUCK!!!" (Thank, God, I was wearing a tank top, had a tan, was wearing makeup, looked cute, and, thankfully, Bob managed to keep his mouth shut!) So I tell him the story of the long hours worked, it was just newly purchased, I was working far from out of where I lived, and that we were just bringing home trees that the quarry that were only going to waste anyway. Then the trooper says, "You are doing other things wrong, also! You need a Class 'A CDL License' to run that hookup along with Combination Plates." (Now, I didn't know anything about Combination Plates, but I DID know that you need a CDL for a tractor trailer.) In my confusion, I politely say to the officer, "Sir, are you joking with me? Because this is just a Dodge Ram 3500 with a trailer behind it." "Yes, miss, I AM serious." he says. Then I repeatedly asked him again if this was a joke. (It was like my mind transformed into some kind of robot with damaged cerebral circuitry causing me to reiterate myself, trying to function in my horror!) So I say, "Sir, this isn't even a tractor trailer, it's just a truck and a trailer, and I don't even know what Combination Plates are!" Then he calmly explains to me that you need a CDL for any trailer with a Gross Vehicle Weight at 15,000 pounds, and the plates would link the truck to the trailer's weight. What? WHAT?!?

Now my emotions shifted gears from terror to total enragement! (And here is a weird problem I have in life;

sometimes the angrier I get, the funnier I get! This always pissed me off growing up, because sometimes in my adolescence, I would start ranting to my stepdad about something or other, and instead of being sympathetic to my plight, he would start rolling laughing, which would do nothing but to serve to piss me off even more! "Stop laughing, you asshole, this isn't frigging funny!" I would shriek! "Yes, YES, it is!" he would choke! But then the two of us would end up giggling, and it was the most bizarre parental guidance ever thought possible!)

So I start screaming, "THOSE SONS OF BITCHES THAT SOLD ME THE TRAILER AT THAT COMPANY NEVER FUCKING TOLD ME THAT!!! I'M GOING TO KILL THIS THING!" I then launch myself on the side of it with supernatural skills of both speed and agility (and quite possibly, hormonal monthly elevations and/or the fact that I was sober and, therefore, completely psychotic), and start pounding the floorboards with my fists, and kicking the tires with my boots! Astounded and shocked by my unanticipated actions, the trooper grabs my waist and my husband grabs my feet! Suddenly, I was completely horizontal by this point, but still managed to keep a death grip on this potential mechanical roadkill! Bob starts screaming, "BE CAREFUL! SHE'S QUICK LIKE A FERRET...AND SHE SOMETIMES BITES!" I'm still shrieking, "I WILL MURDER THIS PIECE OF SHIT! I HOPE IT DIES! I WILL TAKE IT HOME AND BURN IT! AND I HOPE IT GOES TO SOME AUTOMOTIVE HELL FOR AN ETERNITY, WHERE ITS WHEELS DRYROT, ITS FRAME RUSTS APART, ITS BRAKES SEIZE UP, ITS

## REFLECTIVE TAPE TURNS INTO PLAID, AND WEASELS EAT ALL ITS WIRING HARNESSES OFF!

I was very small at the time, but I was also very strong! I put on one spectacular show, until an equally spectacular tug from the two wrestlers managed to pop me off the side, sending me flying onto the ground with the velocity of a 200 MPH of some cheap Champagne cork being discharged in some shitty New Year's Eve Party! It was like drop kicking a hedgehog on a football field! I curled up like one in midflight, before bouncing to a stop! Then, instead of using a taser on my ass, the trooper does the funniest thing ever! He backs up against the guiderail, AND BURSTS OUT LAUGHING! I am still stuck curled up in the fetal position, with dirt in my hair, grass strains on my clothes, and brush burns on my arms. I start screaming, "I HATE BOTH OF YOU MORE THAN THAT FUCKING TRAILER NOW!" Then I cracked up laughing, too! Now my husband starts laughing, also! Thank, God, no passers had managed to capture this ridiculous display of insanity!

After we all composed ourselves, the trooper says the nicest thing ever. "Honey, that company basically didn't disclose any of those facts, because they were just trying make a sale. They probably would have sold a freezer to an Eskimo, if they could have. I have a part time landscaping business, and the same thing happened to me with my trailer once!"

This guy could've been a real dick and called DOT in or fined us terribly, but he was completely enthralled with this trailer! He had never seen a gooseneck one before. If you are unfamiliar with these, let me enlighten you (much like the education I gave the statey that day). Normal trailers hook up behind a truck bumper, but these actually lock into a ball on a plate inside your truck's bed. This means that you can carry a little bit more weight on them, and they ride more smoothly than conventional trailers when shifting gears. This trooper was so curious how this setup worked, that he bounces over the bed of the truck, AND FALLS INTO BOB'S SEA OF BEER CANS! "OH MY FUCKING, GOD! MY HUBAND IS A TOTAL FUCKING IDIOT" I silently scream! IF YOU'RE GOING TO DO SOMETHING KNOWINGLY ILLEGAL, TRY NOT AND BE SO STUPID ABOUT IT!!! I COULD FEEL MYSELF DYING INSIDE!!

Instead of issuing a DUI, this officer kicks this aluminum wasteland aside, and starts excitedly checking out this hookup! What was even going on around here?!? "This is the coolest thing I've ever seen!" he exclaims! "This is the worst thing I've ever seen!" I mentally shriek!

But once again, the officer is incredibly outgoing! He says, "Listen, you two just be careful, get home safely, AND PUT A GOD DAMN PLATE ON THIS THING!" Mr. State Trooper/Part Time Landscaper/and Compassionate Soul, I LOVE YOU! AND I HAVE MARRIED THE WRONG PERSON! Are you single?!?

Here is another weird story involving vehicles when sobriety actually occurred. When it was the 90's, I had this awesome teal green Mustang with ground effects. (This wasn't the dumber, rounder model that this company has managed to puke out nowadays.) Anyways, I always buy

"R Titles" because they are cheaper, and still drive the same. This means that they have been in a wreck once, but some garage has managed to refurbish them. So oneday, I am getting gas down at the local station. I slammed my door, and that's when the explosion happened! Suddenly, I was knocked over into the passenger seat, the car was filled with smoke, and I couldn't see out of my left eye, or hear out of my left ear! Thinking that I was car jacked, and had got shot in the side of the head, I laid there for a few seconds. Then the other Vaness calmly spoke to me. "Put your hand against the side of your head, and see how much brain matter is leaking out! (Probably not much, ever, in my humble opinion!) But I wasn't bleeding anywhere!

The next thing I knew, some Good Samaritan was dragging me out of my car, screaming, "JESUS CHRIST, HONEY, ARE YOU OK?!? YOUR FUCKING AIR BAG JUST WENT OFF!" Oh, golly, is that what just happened? All my sensory perceptions were completely useless at point in time! As a side note, in the commercials involving these apparatuses, they appear to be portrayed like fluffy white pillow cases being deployed to save your life. But this is the real truth. They are like getting hit in the face with a basketball being launched from a cannon at two hundred miles per hour! I'd rather have my face put through my windshield and spend the next day picking glass out of it than ever to get hit with one of these ever again! Fuck, did that hurt! (Thank God that I didn't have a cigarette or a lollipop in mouth. I would have to try and pick either out of my throat!)

The next day at work, my face was all black and blue! So I call the car dealership screaming to fix this automotive abortion! They were actually very good about it, until I screeched that I wanted this this device dismantled! "I don't think that's legal!" the mechanic says! "I SWEAR TO GOD, THIS CAR WILL ROT THERE UNTIL YOU FIX THE STEERING WHEEL AND PULL THE FUSE! YOU, ASSHOLE!" I shriek! "OK, OK!" he screams! Well, long story short, it was fixed the way I wanted it! No more driving in terror! Slamming car doors did not horrify me anymore!

But here is the other time this car tried to kill me AND MY FAMILY! It was like "Christine" in Stephen King's novel! Growing up, I was really into car stereo and speaker systems. I realize this is a weird hobby for a girl, but aside from collecting unicorn statues, this really amused me! Oh, what kind of booming sound system could I install in this sexy beast this month? A six disk CD player, another amplifier, or bigger Pyle Driver speakers? OH, this pastime gave me so much pleasure! Then I would go cruising around after school and work, thumping away!

Anyway, one day I was working on this car in my parents' garage when I hear a small "POP!" I really didn't know what the noise was at first, until the smoldering started under the dashboard! MY CAR WAS ON FIRE! Now, thank God my brother was home, because I completely lose control! "Get the hose I scream!" "No! Not the hose he screams! This is an electrical fire!" And then he tackles me! What the hell was really going on here?!? My car is smoldering in my house, my brother has me pinned to the ground, OH GOD, DID I HAPPEN MENTION THAT MY CAR WAS BURNING?!? Most kids get grounded for throwing keg parties on the weekends when their parents weren't home. Well, I accidentally managed to almost burn the house down, SOBER!

Thankfully, one of us was capable in Damage Control, and it was my brother! He pops the hood open, disconnects the battery, and then puts the fire out with a towel with a calmness that would rival some Indian Buddhist! Then we both stood there in silence, trying to assess this travesty. We actually stood there for quite a while just staring at the smoking wreckage, before he says, "Well, let's see if this if this bitch still runs!" And by Jesus, it still did!

This is what happened. When I was installing my next upgrade of stereo, I managed to bump the wire for the fog lights, which were directly connected to the battery, without a fuse! Now I'm just a woman, BUT I KNOW THAT EVERYTHING ELECTRICAL NEEDS A FUSE! It might be something in your house that needs a breaker panel, or something in your vehicle that needs to be connected to the fuse box or an in line fuse installed. Fuses are important! What was with this mechanic who worked on this car?!? Thank you, Sally Struthers School of Mechanical Engineering! Now MY fuse of patience blew with his inadequate skills!!!

Other weird stories involving traffic accidents of terrible atrocities! One morning, I am driving to a construction site in the dark through a major State Route when I am in the slow lane, because there was absolutely no traffic. This actually saved my life, because I have a terrible habit of not wearing my seat belt. (This is nothing to be proud of, but after my former torment of safety devices, I have an incredible mistrust for them!) I lean over to turn the radio on, when I think I catch headlights going past me! Was I that overtired, or just still half in the bag from the night before?!? Stupid alluring and intoxicating effects of red wine! Stupid fermented grapes! Stupid me for imbibing so much!

Anyway, I get to work and turn on the radio on in my truck, where I proceed to hear the announcer say that some idiot got on the wrong ramp of Route 81, and managed to take out four cars! THIS WAS THE SAME SAID IDIOT THAT FLEW BY ME! How did I manage to avoid that head on collision?!? AND THIS GUY WAS ABSOLUTELY SOBER! I might drive around half shitted up most of time, but if I realize if all the state signs are facing in the wrong direction, THAT I AM IN THE WRONG FUCKING LANE! Jesus Christ, how people could be such morons?!? Always, drive the bigger truck, folks, because if you get hit head on, you'll never feel anything! (Unless that nasty air bag decides to deploy! Then you are definitely screwed!) That's why I always left the plow frame on this beast! I could hit a stone wall going a hundred miles an hour, and I never had to worry about another one of these things ingloriously punching me in the face ever again!

# Other Stories Involving Directional Impairment

I cannot actually bitch about this guy being confused (although I'm sure the drivers hit behind me did!) But one time, I did manage to lose my aunt at a hospital! She goes in for minor surgery, and I slip out for a smoke. (This was yet ANOTHER terrible decision on my part!) I take the elevator, but there is no ground floor! I get out, and start wandering about aimlessly, looking for assistance. I finally find a nice girl that tells me that I have to take the same elevator system back to the original floor, and then find the other one that leads to the ground floor. WHAT?!? Then she says the sweetest thing, "Dear, I have worked here for three months, and I still get lost, seriously!" So I continue on my quest for nicotine!

I finally escape this facility to inhale. Apparently, you are not allowed to smoke in front of a hospital. I personally find this practice a little absurd, because if you are suddenly stricken with lung cancer or emphysema, YOU ARE ALREADY AT A HOSPITAL! A bunch of construction workers escort me down to a street corner, and tell me that I could smoke there. Then the real weirdness started to happen! I was mistaken for a hooker, and I was not even scantily clad! Some older guy stops next to me, and asks me how much for a good time! I lean in his car window, look at him dead seriously, and say evilly, "That depends on what you're looking for!" His sleazy demeanor suddenly shifted gears from sexual prowess into terror, and he sped off! (Maybe he just hated smokers!)

Now I go back into the hospital, where I head to Level 5 for room 556. This is where I am told that there is no Room 556...WHAT THE FUCK WAS GOING ON AROUND HERE ALREADY?!? I was told that there was ANOTHER Level 5 on A DIFFERENT WING! All I had to do, was take the elevator system around the corner to Level 3 and then take the corridor around to the next elevator that would take me up to the OTHER Level 5. WHAT?!? How many more elevator systems could this place possibly have?!? And why not give this area a different level number? Was everyone here only capable of counting to five?!?

At this point in time, all of my mental capacity for dealing with general insanity basically disintegrated. Terrible ideas started going through my mind! For starters, I thought that maybe my family was sick and tired of my instability and had institutionalized me! I was probably hopped up on Thorazine and would be trapped in this hellacious labyrinth forever! What was I doing again? OH, I know, I was looking for my aunt! Then the unthinkable happened! I wondered if this was just a complete nightmare! For years after college I was assaulted with ones that I could not remember what course schedules I was supposed to take and at what times. I would dream that I would have to go into the front office, and shamefully have to admit that I had no clue where I was supposed to be! And where was my aunt supposed to be, either?!? I felt like I was trapped in that M.C. Escher drawing with all the staircases! Or maybe an episode of The Twilight Zone! WHAT PSYCHOTIC GROUP OF ENGINEERS HAD MANAGED TO DESIGN THIS PLACE?!? After what seemed like an arduous three hour trek consuming me in utter terror, I finally managed to locate her! "COME ON, PACK YOUR SHIT, WE ARE GETTING OUT OF THIS ASYLUM BEFORE WE ARE TRAPPED HERE FOR ETERNITY! I don't care how you are feeling, let's just get rolling!!!" I scream!

# Other Weird Stories about Being Trapped in Terrible Places

Here is another weird story how my shear laziness almost killed me. The articulate trucks I used to drive didn't have heated mirrors. This sounds like me being a whiner, but when they are covered with sleet, and you are trying to see to back up to an excavator, you could die with one wrong turn! Now, here was the one bad factor, the mirrors are very far away from the cab, so you can't just lean over the seats and wipe them off like in a triaxle. The driver's side was easy to clean, because all you had to do was open the door and bounce out! But the passenger side really sucked because you had walk around the front of the cab on the catwalk, tilted on ice, and TRY NOT TO SLIP OFF AND DIE! And I had to do this EVERY TIME that I backed up! So I devised a plan! (This usually is a strong indicator of an uncoming disaster scenario!) And it was, too! I was tiny enough at the time, so I would open up the passenger window and creep out through it to clean that mirror off as well. This was a great idea, but for one thing. All the controls were on that side! One day, I am half way through it, when the unthinkable happens! My knee hits the shifter lever, and KNOCKS THIS TRUCK INTO GEAR! Now this thing goes rolling downhill WITH ME STILL STUCK IN THE WINDOW! OH JESUS! Thank God for all the sleet, because I eventually managed to slip back into the cab like a greased pig and stop it! Thank you, General Laziness and Ill Designed, Yellow Death Machine for the thirty second heart attack!

# Other Weird Shit Involving Tampons Almost Causing Horrific Auto Accidents and Other Accidents in General

Most people, men and women alike, hear the word tampon and cringe, because they just know they are associated with a terrible array of disaster! Be it emotional, or physical, that of being helplessly surrounded by sharks in a red sea like defenseless bait, everyone is going home crying in this game! Well, I am here to tell you that they can kill! And I'm not talking about Toxic Shock Syndrome, either! One day, my friend is driving his wife's car to work. Her purse must have accidentally opened, freeing one of these Fluffy Angels of Death to go down under the driver's seat. Well, he starts going down this steep hill, when this gremlin of destruction decides to commit homicide to the driver! It goes rolling across the floor, and manages to somehow lodge itself under the brake pedal! Now he's furiously (and fruitlessly) trying to dislodge this stubborn thing! He goes careening out of control down this hill, and blows through the intersection below! He finally manages to get the car under control, before almost wrecking it! This was followed by epic shrieking to his wife on the phone of, "YOU DUMB, BITCH! NEXT TIME KEEP YOUR FUCKING PURSE CLOSED!"

(This is a side note of how I was almost killed by a peach! The same thing happens to me! I am driving to work in the pitch black, eating an overripe peach, when this thing slips out of my hand, and it, too, goes rolling under MY brake pedal! These pedals must have the gravitational force of Saturn with its asteroid belt! I am driving down a major interstate route trying to grab this slimy thing, when I miss my exit! I finally get a hold of this Produce Goblin of Hell and throw it out the window! People, if you are ever trying to locate something in life, whether it be a lost dog, your wallet or purse, or just your sanity in general, try looking under your brake pedal, BECAUSE IT'S PROBABLY FUCKING THERE!!!)

OK, now, back to tampons. Here is the problem. If you are a female, and work in the construction industry like I do, you spend most of your days suffering on jobsites. This means carrying a purse is completely impossible. So you start hiding tampons everywhere like some deranged Easter Bunny hiding eggs! In the work truck glove box, in your desk drawer, and in covert areas on sites, where ever! One day, the cool guy from upstairs, comes down, and starts rifling through my desk looking for paperwork. I just so happened to be there, when I witness him open my tampon drawer! Cotton ponies rolling everywhere! He stands there, speechless for one minute, before saying, "Well, I guess if I accidentally get my period, I'll know where to come!" And then slams the drawer shut, only to continue on to his paperwork search!

I have a terrible habit in life of not understanding reality. So this demented idea occurs to me! I envision putting a vase on my desk, with some kind of floral arrangement around these shameful things! Perhaps some Baby's Breath or exotic ferns could be used to accentuate this display! Maybe special lighting could be used to feature the exotic colors of whatever absorbency of what would be needed, depending whatever time of month it was! I could probably market these things to yuppies everywhere! Hey, is your wife's or girlfriend's birthday or anniversary coming up? Let her know that you THINK you care, by buying one of these decorative, useful pieces! Who needs flowers, when tampons say, "I LOVE YOU," with so much more practicality! For a limited time, I am only offering discounted prices!

One day, I'm on a jobsite, where the unthinkable happens! The Hoover Dam in my system breaks unexpectedly, and lets forth an unfathomable red tide! I had no time to Macgyver anything! My jeans were completely ruined instantaneously! So I tie a shirt around my waist and try to find the most compassionate soul there, which turned out to be a technician. Much like a child terrified, and completely lost from its parents at a mall, I wail, "CAN YOU PLEASE HELP ME?!?" Now, you'd think most guys would be squeamish about this, but we all grew up in the country here, where gutting deer is the norm. He takes one look at me and proclaims, "Don't worry, Vaness! This used to happen to my wife all the time! I have an extra pair of jeans in the back of my truck, and I think we are about the same size." Strangely, they happened to fit me perfectly! (Not that I was concerned about a fashion statement at this particular time, but I have a woman's hips, and that sometimes makes it hard to fit into anything made for a guy!) What a sweetheart!

I wasn't the only girl to ever have this happen to them on a jobsite! This is how my quarry superintendent met his future wife! One day he is in his office, when she bursts in crying, covered in crimson, with a shirt also tied around her waist! Thinking that she was either gut shot or had accidentally impaled herself on something in the quarry, he starts screaming, "JESUS CHRIST! I'LL GET YOU A FUCKING AMBULANCE!" "NO!," she starts wailing, "I JUST WANT TO GO HOME!" And much like instant replay, terrified, he starts screaming again, "JESUS CHRIST! DO YOU NEED A RIDE OR ANYTHING?!?" "NO!" she is still wailing, "I JUST WANT TO GO FUCKING HOME!" Stupid uteruses everywhere that are unmanageable, are unable to adhere to calendars, and have horrific explosion factors, I hope you all die! Screw procreating the human species! Maybe you think that women just need to pay more attention, but someone needs to have an onsite bomb team to diffuse these mischievous, randomly date selective, hellacious deviants! Stupid men, burn in hell for not having one! Well, apparently hemoglobin contains exceptional pheromones, because this couple were married ten years later! (This is the weirdest love story ever, in my opinion!)

# Weird Things Involving Propane and My Rage Disorder

Now, I should have known better, but I started dating this married guy for four years. He offers to take me to my company Christmas Party! Oh, goody, how eager was I? I had really long hair at the time, and had put on a long velvet dress on with feathers on the top. We had a wonderful time, until he started picking fights with me! I knew where this was going! He just didn't want to stay over at my house that night. By the time he dropped me off in my driveway, we were in FULL BLOWN RED CODE ARGUMENTIVE STAGE! He screams, "YOU'RE JUST A STUPID TRUCK DRIVER, WHO MAKES $10.50 AN HOUR!" Well, the gin and tonics I had that night, lead to my low blood sugar, and supernatural strength! BANG! I FUCKING PUNCHED HIM AS HARD AS I COULD, IN HIS FACE! WOW! He didn't see that one coming! (This was actually amazing, because I was REALLY spectacularly, physically fit at the time.) I don't condone domestic violence whatsoever, but sometimes, some places, PEOPLE JUST NEED TO SHUT THE FUCK UP! Now I escape to my house, crying uncontrollably.

All I wanted was a cigarette. If you are a smoker, this is the worst thing to happen to you. To have cigarettes AND NO LIGHT! IT'S EVEN WORSE THAN NOT HAVING ANY CIGARETTES AT ALL! I am crying like a little bitch, so I go to light one off the propane stove. I put my face down to the burner, when epic travesty happened! I had not realized how much hairspray I had managed to cover myself with! Both on my hair, and somehow, on my dress! I FUCKING explode in flames everywhere! OH, MY FUCKING, GOD! And I'm not talking a little smoldering here, I WAS ACTUALLY ON FUCKING FIRE! I put the inferno out with a dishrag, the only saving grace to my face, was probably the fact that I was still crying so badly, that the tears managed to save it! THIS FUCKER! That was the end of THAT! This brings me to…

# Weird Shit Involving My Rage Disorder Without Propane

I used to have this one boss who used to say, "I am terrified of you, when I piss you off. The spooky thing is, you will never steal from me or ever even break anything to get back at me. You are just creatively evil, and that is a million more times more horrifying!" So now I hate this guy so much that made me cry, I devise a plan! His favorite thing in life was his black 1500 Dodge Ram. I go down to the Dodge dealership and completely describe this guy's truck, AND THEN I TELL THEM I WANT SOMETHING BIGGER! "We can get you a 2500" they exclaim! "No, I want something bigger!" I retort! "We can get you a 2500 diesel!" They say! "But it will cost five grand more, and have slightly different colors." I scream that I don't care about the price, but it has got to look EXACTLY like this other truck! Find me one, someplace, somewhere, in this country! The salesperson looks me dead in the eye and says, "You are a woman scorned, aren't you?" Yes, I indeed was, and the equity loan I took out on my house to pay for this pig proved it! But it was all worth it! Because one day, on the way home from work, I run into him! The look on his face when he saw me pull up next to him with a bigger, badder truck, was priceless! It was well worth paying that 30 year loan back! And the funny thing is, because I paid it off with my loan, I already had the TITLE! I showed it to this guy, and REALLY fucked with his head! Boy, this was awesome revenge!

# More Weird Shit Involving Vehicles that I Actually Had Nothing to Do With (for Once)

One day, I am working with this technician, who tells me the funniest story ever! When he was young, he was in charge of a bunch of nuclear power plants. So one Friday, a forlorn employee comes over to his house and asks to borrow the company truck so he can cash his paycheck at the bank. This nice guy says, "Sure," and tosses him the keys. (By the way, this is how all of us "NICE" people end up screwing ourselves, BY BEING FUCKING NICE IN THE FIRST PLACE! Also, please keep in mind that this story was before cell phones were invented.) So this guy leaves, AND COMPLETELY DISAPPEARS! Now the manager is calling this idiot's house for hours, AND FINALLY GETS A HOLD OF HIM! Said idiot says that he has no idea what has happened to the truck, or where it could quite possibly be! This is where the manager tells me, "Vaness, I was so horrified, that a complete moment of calmness enveloped me." "Do you even remember the last place you were remotely at?!?" he asks Braindead. "No!" Braindead answers! So there begins this manager's epic journey of trying to locate this mechanical pony in the hopes of not getting fired!

Now, I think this was a pretty well devised plan! He starts out at the bank, and makes a tight rotation around every bar henceforth! (Unfortunately, this is where his plan went south!) Much like his assclown employee, he has a beer at every tavern he stops at! At about three in the morning, and after absorbing much alcohol, he gets a great idea! Call the police station, and ask if it was towed! (This is like something I would do, but usually, I am capable of much more dumber things, on a much more grander scale!) Well, the truck was towed, and was indeed impounded! This poor manager has to drive into work the next day taking his car, almost like doing, "The Walk of Shame," after a one night stand! Watch those keys, people!

# More Weird Shit Involving Propane and Not Trucks

One day, my husband and I get home from work, and go to light the wood burner, WHEN I SUDDENLY CAN'T STOP SMELLING PROPANE! Thankfully, the wood burner was being crabby, and neither one of us lit a cigarette yet, BECAUSE I KEPT SMELLING PROPANE! Now, sometimes when your tank runs out, you will get an errant stink throughout your house, BUT THIS WAS MUCH, MUCH WORSE! So, thinking that he had accidentally left the tank on the in the grill, I go and check it, but it's shut off! WHAT THE HELL?!? So then the horror occurred to me! I go creeping out to the backyard, where our tank was, only to discover epic devastation! It had rained a lot that day, and apparently, our tank managed to dislodge itself from the woods, snap off its copper line, and go rolling over the embankment! OH MY FUCKING, GOD! I go racing back into the house, and wrestle Bob's Nudeports off of him! "DON'T LIGHT ANYTHING!" I scream! I tell him what happened, quickly, whereas he runs to assess the scenario, and also shrieks, "OH MY FUCKING, GOD!" Then he at least had the common sense to shut the valve off! The whole yard was one sea of eye watering atmospheric realm of gaseous nuclear fallout!

Now, if you've ever done construction, you are forced to take many painful MSHA classes. You would have at least been subjected to at least one film involving a fire extinguisher being bumped by a forklift, and blowing through a concrete wall, probably maiming some poor unsuspecting employee on the other side! Now I have a potential bomb outside, which I'm pretty sure was capable of exploding at 12,000 kilotons of force rivaling that of throwing a lit cigarette into a case of TNT! So I call the propane place, which was closed at the time. Then I call their emergency hotline, which some tool answers. "Are you sure this is an emergency?" the guy stupidly asks, whereas I retort, "WELL, I DON'T KNOW THE EXACT DENSITY OF THE METAL OF THE WAY THESE TANKS ARE DESIGNED, AND I DON'T SEE ANY DENTS, BUT CERTAINLY DO NOT NEED THIS THING LAUNCHING ITSELF SIDEWAYS THROUGH MY BASEMENT WALL LIKE A ROCKET SHIP WITH ILL FATED COORDINATES AND FIERCE TRAJECTORY POWERS! AND I CERTAINLY DO NOT NEED THIS THING EXPLODING, AND HAVING THE SHRAPNEL KILL EVERYONE IN MY COUNTY, MYSELF INCLUDED!!!

"Just don't light any cigarettes or your wood burner," I am calmly told by this useless droid. Thank you, you FUCKING GENUIS! "We'll send a technician out in the morning." A technician?!? THEY WERE GOING TO NEED A WHOLE FUCKING EXCAVATION CREW

TO FIX THIS MESS! I'm not sure what they did, though, because the next day I come home from work, and this fallen, white lozenge was erected back to its original spot! The only problem was, these idiots managed to put it on cinder blocks once again! AND THIS IS WHY THE PROBLEM HAPPENED THE FIRST FUCKING TIME AROUND! THANK YOU BRAINLESS SERVICE PEOPLE EVERYWHERE!

# More Weird Shit Involving Propane AND a Water Heater

If you have ever lived in the country, you will probably have a well pump. This has its good points and bad points. On the upside, you don't have a water bill like you have to deal with in the city, but on the downside, if this thing shits the bed, YOU HAVE ABSOLUTELY NO FUCKING WATER! Well, that's what happened! So I knew enough to go downstairs and shut the water heater off, so it didn't fry itself. Now, after the epic disaster of trying to replace this pump, which involved much pulling of wires and pipe out of a three hundred foot hole, the accursed one man diving bell was finally replaced. Good times people! Really!

I always try and think ahead. The power goes out a lot where I live, so I special order this 60 gallon water heater that just runs off of propane WITH NO ELECTRIC WHATSOEVER when I bought my house! This meant that if I had no electricity, I could still drain the tank and take a quick, hot bath in the morning before work. So after a week of having no water and eventually showering at the neighbor's house, I was actually delighted to do all the dishes in the sink that had managed to accumulate! I am in the kitchen trying to get things situated, and my husband goes downstairs to try and relight this thing. In retrospect, I should have reversed our roles, and none of the disaster would have occurred! In the back of my head I could hear him down there, but apparently my subconscious compass for locating stupidity was broken that day. Click click. Click click. Click click. Click click. Click click. Click click. I am still upstairs rearranging dishes. Now, everyone knows if you try and start a propane water heater repeatedly, and it doesn't start, to let the fumes air out after a few tries. Well, NOT BOB! Click click. Click click. Click click. Click click. Click click. FUCKING KABOOM! I SWEAR TO GOD THE WHOLE FUCKING HOUSE JUMPED A FOOT OFF OF ITS FOUNDATION!

Instantaneously realizing what had happened, I go tearing off downstairs! There is Bob standing there, with his hair blown back, looking like Wile E. Coyote after detonating an ACME bomb! I don't know how every window in the basement did not manage to blow out! Now I notice the REAL DEVISTATION! The top of my precious water heater was blown off and the vent system landed somewhere in the woods about 50 feet away from the house! I go ballistic! "YOU DUMB, MOTHER FUCKER!" I scream, not caring whether he was dying from a concussion or not! So now this situation gets even worse. I go down to the local plumbing place for replacements, and am told, that this was a really odd model I bought, and parts could not be shipped for another two weeks! OH MY FUCKING

GOD! I FINALLY HAVE WATER AGAIN, BUT NO FUCKING HOT WATER! JESUS WEPT! Here's to heating water on the stove, the coffee maker, and in the microwave!

# Weird Things That I Have Done To Even Rival My Husband's Stupidity, Like My Accidental Overdose at Work

Most people, when they think of overdoses, think of illegal drugs. Well, I'm here to tell you, THE SAME THING CAN HAPPEN WITHOUT THEM! One day, I accidentally wake up late for work! This never happens to me! Now, everyone has their own little ritual before work. I used to take a certain amount of a kind of pills to try and quit smoking before I would take my bath in the morning (I would mention the name brand, but no, because who needs a lawsuit here? NOT ME!), but I was terribly discombobulated. So while rushing around like a lunatic, I call my boss, and tell him that I'm going to be a little late, but that I would get us both coffees. He says not to worry, whenever I got there, I got there. So I fly through the hour and half drive, and stop for the coffees. Unfortunately, this is where all the weirdness started to happen. I go to pay for them, and suddenly I can't remember why I am there! Then I start driving to work, and can't remember on and off where I am headed to! I finally get to the office, and then the real fun occurs! I have never done acid before, because my mind is already a twisted place to be, so thinking that particular pharmaceutical would be a terrible choice of drug that would only magnify my already atrocious mental state, I have never indulged upon it. Well, this was the day to confirm exactly why!

I answer the phone, and start stuttering so bad, that I could barely talk. Then the walls just seemed like they looked strange to me. I'm pretty sure that they were melting! Then the horror occurred! In my rush to get ready in the morning, I HAD ACCIDENTALLY TAKEN MY PILLS TWICE! OH GOD, NO!!! 900 MILLIGRAMS! I vanish downstairs to where, thankfully, nobody else was, when the real theatrics happened! I park myself in a chair, helplessly trying to recover! This is when I thought the table was trying to kill me. It's not like I saw eyes and a mouth on it, but I was convinced that the wood grain was going to fly out and carve me up into a million little pieces! I could deal with that, but not when the seizure occurred! I started flailing around like a fish out of water! Thankfully, my compassionate boss happens to come down to use the bathroom before the big meeting upstairs. (Boy, of all days to screw up!)

Well, he showed up just in time, because this is when the table almost DID KILL ME! Even in my incapacitated state, I knew what was about to happen! Having absolutely no motor skills, I started to fall forward and vomit. If he wasn't there to grab me by the hair, I would have smashed my head off of this piece of Ikea shit, probably knocking myself unconscious, and die on the floor, choking on my own puke like a rock star! He's still got me by the hair with one hand

and manages to somehow get his other arm around me to pin down my flipping arms so I wouldn't hurt myself. Then I really did vomit on the floor! (I personally think that this was my body's way of trying to get all of the poison out of my system and save itself!) Oh, such grace!

"JESUS CHRIST, VANESS! I'LL CALL YOU AN AMBULANCE!" he shrieks! "NO!" I scream! "THERE IS A ROOM FULL OF BIGWIGS UP THERE, AND I DON'T WANT TO ATTRACT ANY MORE ATTENTION THAN NECESSARY!" (At least the wiring from my brain to my voice box was still functioning, and I was still capable of SOME kind of reasoning!) "Will YOU please take me to the hospital?!?" I cry!

This poor man truly deserved a medal that day! He goes from an executive business meeting, to carting his incompetent employee to a clinic. Now more terror ensues! I became convinced that once he opened the door to his white, little car, that it was going to eat me like Pac Man! I would have put up a fight, BUT NOW MY LEGS WOULDN'T WORK! That's OK, though, because MY ARMS WERE STILL PICKING UP THE SLACK, RANDOMLY PUNCHING THINGS! He scoops me up, carries me up the stairs, and throws me in the passenger seat. Off to the races! Now I cannot, absolutely, cannot stop swallowing. Being pretty convinced that I was going to choke on my tongue, I start begging him for bottles of water. Well, within 20 minutes I managed to down four. (Apparently in my terror, I semi regained hand dexterity, but there was a lot of aqua splashed on his interior, on his windshield, and all over myself!)

We get to the hospital, where he has to carry me in. Usually, you have to fill out a ton of paperwork, and sit in the waiting room for hours, but the receptionist takes one look at me frothing at the mouth like a rabid dog, and screams, "OH, MY GOD! Put her in one of the back rooms, immediately!" I end up on one of the gurneys, still thrashing about, when Dr. Ratchet enters, and asks if I had overdosed on purpose. This started our ill fated relationship from the get go! "LADY, I THINK IF I WAS GOING TO TRY AND OVERDOSE, I'D SHOOT FOR THE MOON! MAYBE I'D TRY FOR A WHOLE 8 BALL OR A BOTTLE OF ASPRIN! BUT NOT THIS SHIT! JESUS CHRIST, GIVE ME SOME CREDIT HERE! EXTRA POINTS FOR CREATIVITY!" After her stupid interrogations were over, she tells me the dumbest thing ever uttered by a physician. "Well, you can't die from this!" This said to a patient that still had uncontrollable muscle spasms!

This idiotic statement managed to unleash such unholy rage and adrenaline in my system, that both my mind and body somehow miraculously, immediately repaired itself! I slide off the bed, and sit on the chair in the room, where my enragement continued! She keeps on yammering about how there was nothing wrong with me. (What a bitch!) Now the animalistic part in me that's interested in basic survival and is just blatantly pissed off, unleashes an epic torrent of those consumed four bottles of water in my system all over her, the floor, and then the sink! I was like Linda Blair in the Exorcism! I mean, serious projectile vomiting was going on here, kids, and I'm pretty sure that I was turning inside out! I was a terrible tsunami of vomit! Once again, my poor boss has to grab me by the hair!

By the time we left there, he was screaming not at me, but about the doctor! "WHAT A DUMB FUCKING CUNT! I'M GLAD YOU PUKED ON HER BECAUSE I WAS READY TO PUNCH HER IN THE FUCKING FACE!" This strangely was the most comforting thing that could ever be said to me! I never paid the bill there, because I was so pissed off! I eventually did read up on this medication, AND YOU CAN INDEED DIE FROM IT! GRAND MAL SEIZURES AND BRAIN DAMAGE COULD OCCUR! Where did this woman get her degree from? A back of a cereal box?!? Good! I'm glad I puked on her! I wish I could drive back there and barf on her again!

I thought I was the only idiot to do this, but a week later, the other manager accidentally also takes his blood pressure medication twice one morning, and goes down for the count on the jobsite! Thankfully, he was not backed over by a triaxle or squashed by a piece of equipment! Once again, my poor boss has to cart another employee to the hospital! "WHAT AM I? A PROJECT MANAGER, OR A FUCKING AMBULANCE DRIVER?!?" he shrieks! (Well, in my opinion, I think he was very good at both!)

# Weird Shit Involving Motorcycles Not Involving Overdoses

I actually wonder if there is a name for this disorder, because my whole entire life, I will actually almost go into a coma in a moving vehicle. So one of my friends would take me out riding on Sundays. This was a great idea and a lot of fun, until my REM Cycle would set in. I would fall COMPLETELY dead asleep on the back of him! Now, most people would think epic disaster would occur here, but here's the odd thing. Much like a koala bear that has eaten too much eucalyptus, I would latch on to him like a tree bearing such said offerings. And the DEEPER I fell asleep, the tighter I would HOLD ON! (Strangely, NO ALCOHOL OR EVEN LEGAL DRUGS were involved in this tale!) He would drive for hours, avoiding potholes, swerving around corners, AND I WOULD BE DEAD ASLEEP ON THIS BIKE! We would get back to his garage, where he would proclaim, "Vaness, you are the BEST passenger ever! I've given people rides before, but they wiggle so much about, that they almost make me lose my balance. You're dead asleep on the back on this motorcycle, and I don't even know that you are even there!" Now, if you think I'm making this up, I'm not. One day, I'm at a party at his garage, and this other guy starts screaming, "Why does my wife always fall asleep on the back of my bike?!?" Same thing. She would curl up next to him and be out like a light, JUST LIKE ME! Was there some kind syndrome going on here?!? Someone needs to do testing on sleep disorders involving vehicular movement involving this!

# Other Weird Things Involving My Supernatural Strength

I end up working for this same guy who had a spray foam business. This would entail loading barrels of epoxy into the back of his box truck. One day, though, one of them gets stuck trying to get put on a pallet in there. So I watch this poor mechanic struggle for a half hour trying to move this thing. Now, my father always had a terrible temper in life, so I am well versed in two things. If a man is floundering around, do not laugh, because you will get a belting. And do not offer any suggestions, BECAUSE YOU WOULD GET AN EVEN BIGGER BELTING! So I watch this guy suffer for a bit more, when I finally can't take it anymore! I say, "Do you want me to put that barrel on that pallet for you?" Being frustrated, tired, and pissed off, he starts shrieking at me! "Vaness, you are only 120 pounds soaking wet, and the shipping weight of this thing is 550 pounds! That's completely fucking impossible!" I tell him to just catch it in time before it flips over. Then I scoot down on the bottom of the truck, and channeling all my rage disorder, and piston my legs as hard as I could against it! Well, this thing goes flying over the pallet and almost through the other wall of the truck! The mechanic is just standing there speechless. Then he screams, "Jesus Christ! I can't believe I just fucking saw that! Please don't tell anyone that just happened!" Come on, let's just go and do some insulating already!

Here is another story involving my supernatural strength. I used to live with a boyfriend in an apartment for a couple of years. Well, every time he would come home overtired and drunk, he would pee the bed. (Rumor has it, that this is a usual occurrence with guys.) I didn't care, because it was a water bed and easy to wipe down, but the horrible thing was that instead of stripping the covers off so I could wash them, HE WOULD JUST REMAKE THE FUCKING BED LIKE NOTHING EVER HAPPENED!!! So here was the great part! I would get home, dead tired, after working a double shift of second and third, and try to go to sleep. AND SLIDE INTO A SOAKING WET BED! AHHH! How many countless times had this happened?!? Too many! Then one day before Easter, he passes out on my couch, and make the educated guess here, people, of what happened! That's right! HE PISSES ON THAT, TOO! I could deal with the Easy to Clean Bed, BUT NOT MY COUCH! JESUS CHRIST, did I flip out! Thank God for Scotch Guard!

Anyway, he and I ended up breaking up, but not the couch and I! I ended up taking it to my house with me! But years later, this ugly factor never left the back of my mind! There was still pee on it! So one Sunday morning, I get really wacked out on red wine, and lose my temper! That's it! I grab the couch, and drag it through the sliding doors, AND THROW IT OFF A TWO STORY PORCH! (By the way, it's great living in the country. You have absolutely no neighbors to witness your bizarre behaviors! Which is either a good thing or a terribly bad thing, depending on your perspective!) Then I drag out the pressure washer, and hose this thing down! I let it dry, and then dragged it back up the two flights, BY MYSELF! This is where the problem occurred. I COULD NOT GET IT BACK IN THROUGH THE GOD DAMNED SLIDING DOOR! I tried every angle imaginable! Sideways, upside-down, diagonally, you name it! NOTHING! So I go through the back door, and have another glass of wine. Apparently, all that was needed was a little lubrication on my part, because with a pull, this foam tyrant sailed right through this glass guardian gateway, granting me permission to drag it back to its original position. Why, oh, why, do I do the things that I do?!? I didn't care! My couch was probably going to be eventually mold covered, but it was finally pee free!

# Weird Things Involving Terrible Landlords that I Should Have Used My Supernatural Strength On

Now, when I had my apartment, it was a giant complex with a whole bunch of other apartments linked together. Everyone had to pay their own electric bill, but the water meter ran everyone's usage, and the landlord paid that. Pee Master and I had broken up at the time, so I was living there by myself. And considering the fact that I was working double shifts at the time and plus going to school, I was living everywhere BUT there! The landlord gets a bug up his ass about the amount of water usage there, and starts raiding everyone's apartments. This was very easy to do with mine, BECAUSE I WAS NEVER, EVER THERE! Then he finds the unthinkable! I have a little, portable washer in my kitchen! An epic argument ensues between us! I was the one using all the water! I try to politely explain to him that although I had one, and always paid the rent on time, I WAS NEVER EVEN THERE TO USE IT! I am not one of these women who have to wash a towel every time I used one! I would wear the same jeans for days, just as long as they weren't filthy! Then I proceed to tell this gentleman, that there are families of eight living in these places, all flushing the toilets and taking showers, AND NOW THEY ARE HAVING THEIR KIDS' FRIENDS OVER, DOING THE EXACT SAME THING! WHAT'S THE MUTIPLYING FACTOR AROUND HERE, FOLKS?!? HOW THE HELL DID THE LITTLE PORTABLE WASHER THAT WAS USED ONCE A WEEK MANAGE TO COMPARE WITH EPIC WATER USAGE BY THE WHOLE OF AREA LIKEIWANNA COUNTY?!?

Now, this argument really starts evolving! This landlord really gets into it with me! He starts coming into my apartment unexpectedly (apparently this is an accepted practice in PA), and tries to harass me about this issue! This was a terrible idea on his part, for several reasons. Number 1, There was nothing in my lease which specifically said that I could not own this appliance. Number 2, When it was really hot, I would just sleep naked, which I think would probably get him for sexual assault issues. Number 3, Being blind without my contacts in, owning a hand gun, and barely thinking in a sleep deprived state are not a good combination! Number 4, I am a crafty, evil bitch when I am very tired. (Also, sometimes when I am fully awake, but that is really far in few in between!)

So now one morning, he comes busting in and once again scares the SHIT OUT OF ME WHILE I WAS SLEEPING! THAT'S IT, FOLKS! I calmly let him finish his rant, and then say, "Listen, I'll make you an offer. I'll put my washer out on the front lawn tomorrow with a sign on it that says,

"For Sale," but here's the deal. I'm going to change the locks on the doors, and then if you think I'm the one using all the water here, I really will be! When I leave for my 16 hour work day, and then for my additional 2 hour schooling, I am going to bend the lever for the toilet tank so it never stops running, turn on the kitchen sink, and then fire up the shower! AND LET EVERYTHING CONTINUOUSLY RUN WHILE I AM GONE! And now because the weather is cold, and I suddenly stop paying my rent, you can't evict me." (Ah, so now I am ALSO using the legal PA system!)

These ideas completely abhorred this man! Now, I have noticed one thing in life. If you scream at someone, you are getting nowhere, but if you use a very calm, spooky ass, hypnotic voice, you will actually terrify them into obeying you. "Fine!" he screams, "You keep your God Damn washer already!"

Finally, when I put in my notice to end my lease after two years, he tells me that I was the best tenant that he ever had! My apartment was immaculate! The dove grey carpeting still was flawless, the walls were perfect, and I always paid my rent on time! But here was the problem, I had to spend 3 months chasing this ass clown around for my deposit back! I should have taken that washer and blocked in his front door with it! What a dick!

# Other Weird Things Involving Places I've Had to Stay

Now, one would think that because I am a construction worker, I would either be running a piece of equipment or at least using a tape measure, but no. This involved me having to drive to distant hotels to take tests for various certifications. REPEATEDLY! This really sucked because I have no sense of direction, even with Garmin stuck to my windshield. Also, my social anxiety disorder made things worse, because, much like a gold fish being thrown out of its fish bowl onto the floor, I had a hard time functioning outside of my safe zone.

The only redeeming value was that although strangers scared me, I was really, easily amused. I only have a wood burner at home to heat the house. This unit only comes with two settings: Freezing, because it was out, or Blazing Inferno because it was running. So while studying, I would delight myself with the thermostat! Such technological wonders! Between reading asphalt and concrete specs, I would turn the room up to 80, then to 65, then to 80 again, repeatedly!

Most students were either at the bar or watching TV, but I was totally engrossed with this little device!

The worst place I ever stayed at for classes, was a really fancy hotel. Upon arrival, I was told that only valet parking was available. Now, I get horribly attached to inanimate objects (I think with a sneaking suspicion, that this is because they have no emotion, and therefore will never leave me), and so I love this car. It's old, nothing works in it anymore – the sunroof, the windows, the power seats, anything! BUT I STILL LOVED IT, AND NOW STRANGE PEOPLE WERE TAKING IT AWAY FROM ME! Also, I used it as a giant purse, throwing all kinds of extraneous crap in it for work – clothing, paperwork, a deli platter, a gun, etc! And now they were taking it to some underground morgue! What if it was just as scared as I was being trapped with other strange vehicles?!? Could visitation rights be arranged? It was the only friend I had there, and now it was gone!!!

Now I enter this establishment, to find marble floors, marble columns, and gorgeous chandeliers. All these high class, nicely dressed business people were mulling about. And this just made me more panic stricken! I don't belong here, and neither does my car! Until I saw my room. How could a hotel with such a grand entrance, have such shitty rooms?!? I didn't even have a fucking refrigerator! So now I have to play white trash and fill up the sink with ice and put my leftovers on it with a towel over them! Then the truly unthinkable happens! The thermostat has a lock on it, and it's stuck on 68. OH THAT'S IT! GAME ON! HOTEL SHINING, YOU WANT TO SAVE 5 DOLLARS IN

HEAT, NOT GIVE ME AN EXTRA BLANKET, AND RUIN MY FAVORITE PASTTIME, I'LL SHOW YOU!!! I go into the bathroom, and turn the shower on the hottest heat setting there was, and left it there ALL NIGHT LONG WITH THE BATHROOM DOOR OPEN WHILE STUDYING JUST TO HEAT THE ROOM! I'm not really sure how these places are equipped to heat their water. Maybe they have 10,000 gallon tanks for each floor heated by underground volcanic sources. I'm truly not sure, but it managed to run THE WHOLE TIME WITHOUT RUNNING OUT OF HOT WATER! And now my most terrible fear happens! The windows don't open! I'm not really sure why this upsets me. Perhaps I died in "The Towering Inferno," in a past life, because I always need to know where an escape route is! I don't even care if there's a four story drop, because everyone knows that you can't use the elevators in a disaster. You need to use the staircases. But does anyone even pay attention to where these things are located?!? I know that I don't! Because they are never even remotely located to where the elevators are! I live in the country, where I live in a little house. I have three doors on it, so in case of an alert of an impending flaming meteor going to hit it, I always have multiple ways of exit!

Now in the morning, I go down to the restaurant to have breakfast there, when I encounter the weirdest design in carpeting anywhere! It looked like a major acid trip! What the hell kind of designer could have possibly created this?!? So this polite black guy comes over to wait on me. (By the way, I am not prejudice, but I AM a shitty typist, so instead of you being African American and me being a Polish,

Slovak, we are just going to be black and white individuals from here on out!!! Sorry, folks!) I tell him that I'm pretty sure that the carpeting has managed to eat my boots and that I will be probably be immobilized from that table for the rest of the day!

Now he starts laughing and asks me if I want to hear a funny story. SURE, WHO DOESN'T? He tells me that the carpeting has been the original lining from the 70's. (Well, that explains a lot right there.) Then he tells me that one night, he goes to serve this older lady, and she starts shrieking that she couldn't eat, because the carpeting was terrifying her! Now the two of us are laughing so bad about this story, that he actually gave me my breakfast for free! But I tipped greatly that day, and I also got my car back! All things black are great! People, cars, coal, you name it!

Then I get stuck at another shitty hotel going for yet another shitty certification. This place was great in the respect that no one took my car this time, but on the downside, they had no restaurant there. This pisses me off because when I study, I like to just wander downstairs, and grab something. I am really not a big eater, but when I do get hungry, my sugar gets very low, AND I GET VERY ANGRY! So I check my phone for restaurants. (I'm actually very terrible at the phone thing, but starvation is a wonderful motivator!)

Now, here was the weird thing. One would think that staying next to a college campus, that there would be a multitude of places to eat for the students, but there was ABSOLUTELY NOTHING! (Maybe I was doing the wrong profession in life! Maybe it would have eventually been more lucrative if I opened up a pizza joint there!) So I find this barbeque chicken place on my phone, and head there. Once again, this was a terrible decision on my part! (Why do I have such bad luck?) Apparently, this was the bad the bad side of town there! Apparently, also, EVERYWHERE WAS THE BAD SIDE OF TOWN HERE!

The nice black owner grabs me while I was ordering, and starts shaking me like a dog with a toy! "What are you doing here, honey?!? Please, PLEASE tell me that you didn't walk here, because you will get killed on your way back to where ever you are staying!" Get killed on my way back? I thought I was going to die right there! I JUST WANTED CHICKEN, NOT A DEATH SENTENCE! So, now I am upset, and ask him if he sells any alcohol there. (If I'm going to die, it had better be a happy death, at least!) He tells me no, but that there is a bar across the street. So now I go outside, and can't find anything!

Bars where I live, all look inviting! They all have neon signs on them, and plenty of cars parked haphazardly in their parking lots! The only thing I could find, was some warehouse next door hermetically sealed up with plywood over the windows and a steel front door! So, assuming this was the place, I make my grand entrance!

This was a terrible idea. (What's your count up to now on stupidity just in general, Vaness?!? I hope someone was keeping track! Because I surely wasn't!) I walk into this dive, and am surrounded in the dark by people who were actually darker than the dark atmosphere! I stroll into this place, and I was probably so white, that I was neon! Everyone stops what they are doing, and just stare at me. The only thing I could think of, was the restaurant owner was incredibly right! I was going to die in this town! All I could see was eyes and teeth! (Now, I am not prejudice, I really don't care if you're black, white, Jewish or even a Muslim, I will get along with you, just as long as you were nice to me, but this owner had me terrified!) I felt like I was in the "Cantina," in Star Wars! But strangely, immediately everyone goes back to their own affairs, leaving me to order. I go up to the bar, and this is where fear lead to confusion. They didn't serve any regular beer here, just malt liquor. I just grabbed some generic six pack and returned for my chicken order, and then back to my hotel room. This is where even more horror ensued. Apparently, malt liquor makes me very drunk. And I mean very, VERY DRUNK! I can drink vodka and gin like there's no tomorrow, but malt beer crushes me! No great amount of studying was done that night, and I NEVER, EVER screw around when I take these tests!

Now, if you think I am prejudice, I am DEFINITELY NOT! I was on a jobsite once, where I was eating lunch with a bunch of black gentlemen from Sudan, joking around, when one of them tells a weird story. There are three headed Cobras where he came from! "Are you just teasing me just because I'm white?" I laughingly ask. "No, miss, it's true!" everyone of them chime in! This joke drove me crazy until I got home that night, looked it up, and realized that IT WASN'T A JOKE! These things really do exist, AND SOME OF THEM HAVE EVEN MORE THAN THREE HEADS! (No wonder why these guys immigrated!) This lead to utter confusion on my understanding of these slithering reptiles! Which head decided where they were going that day? Who would be actually be in charge? (However, regardless, I'm sure that they would somehow be better coordinated than half of the DOT workers on the roadsides!) And, anyway, if one of them only ate, did the others feel full? What if one of them was a woman and was trapped with a whole bunch of guys, like me? What if one of them hated another's personality and decided to bite and kill him? Would all of them die, or just the offender? (Because I know if you morphed my brother and I together like Siamese Twins, DEFINITELY ONE OF US WOULD BE DEAD BEFORE SUNDOWN!) The next day I'm eating lunch with these guys, and I start laughing about this tale! "See, we told you, miss!" they said!

Now, I loved these black guys for a multitude of reasons. Firstly, they all had great stories from where they came from. Some of them were happy and some of them were sad, but they were ALL INCREDIBLE! Secondly, they were the sweetest people ever! At lunchtime, bored by our prepacked meals, we would trade food around. We would ask "Who wants a few apples for some grapes? Who wants some olives for some pickles? Who wants some deviled eggs for a cantaloupe?" and then we would just end sharing our lunches! It was like some twisted Thanksgiving! Thirdly, though, they all called me miss. I am in my 40's now, and feel old. Everyone around there kept calling me miss, which made me feel young again! Everyone else I deal with calls me ma'am, which makes me feel the exact opposite, OLD! At first, I thought it was a language barrier, but then I realized that most of these guys were trilingual!

I finally snap, and start screaming at them one day during lunch, "All of you people are too smart to be working here! Your company doesn't barely pay you anything, and you ALL could be working as interpreters making a lot more, and not be destroying your bodies with this God Damn, bullshit construction business!!!" Then the leader says, "But, Vaness, this is what we like to do!" Hell, I tried to help!

Then one day, I am working with this crazy white guy who tells me not to open his lunchbox because there was a baby copperhead in it! Thinking that he was teasing me, too, I open Pandora's box to INDEED FIND A COPPERHEAD SNAKE! WHO PUTS SOMETHING LIKE THIS IN THEIR LUNCHBOX?!? "What the hell?!?" I scream! "I told you not to open it." he calmly says. "I found him on a jobsite yesterday. I didn't want him to get hurt, so I picked him up really quick behind his head, and threw him in there. I'm going to release him on this different jobsite today, so he has a better chance of survival." (What was this guy? Part mongoose?) That was a great idea! NOW I PROBABLY WOULDN'T SURVIVE INSTEAD! No more food exchanges around here!

# Terrible Weird Things Involving Food at Places that I Have Either Bartended at or Waitressed at that Don't Involve Poisonous Snakes

Whatever you do in life, do not, AND I ABSOLUTELY MEAN DO NOT, IS PISS YOUR SERVER OFF! Do not bitch about if your meal is undercooked, cold, or not seasoned to your tastes! Because, first off all, it's usually the cook's fault, not your server's. Secondly, this is a very mentally draining job, and in my opinion, unless you have a lobotomy, it is a completely unmanageable task! If you think this profession is a lucrative career choice, most of us would just spend our tips on antidepressants or drugs (or just drink heavily in general), which ever vice was more accessible, just to make it through our shifts!

I once bartended with this older gal, Nancy, who would proclaim before every shift, "I just can't deal with anyone, anymore!" Then she would take two Valium, pour herself a scotch, and then light up a Pall Mall, RIGHT IN FRONT OF THE OWNER! He would always laugh, and say, "Honey, do whatever it takes!"

People who have never had to wait on other people in life, are basically just total assholes. Did you ever stop and compassionately think that half the wait staff called off, that the cook is high on weed and has managed to screw up half the orders, or that the bus boy hasn't cleaned off any of the tables yet BECAUSE HE'S OUT SMOKING POT WITH THE COOK? DID YOU?!? And guess what happens. Shit rolls downhill! Guess who gets to be the whipping boy? Your fucking server!

But we will get you back, people! I used to work at one bar where I would announce on a slow night, that I was shutting the fryer off; would anyone care for anything before I did so? Everyone would decline, but there would always be one errant drunken dick that would wait until it cooled off and then order wings. Now, if you are unfamiliar with these appliances, if you try and cook something with them half warm, the food will absorb all the grease, and come out like goo. And this was an older model that took twice as long to heat up. So this is where I would turn the kitchen into a racquetball court! Wings slammed off the walls, off the appliances, off the cabinets, I think a few cockroaches may have even actually raped a few! YOU NAME IT! "FUCK YOU, YOU COCKSUCKER!" I would silently scream! Mostly, I would just throw them, but sometimes, I would get creative, and just kick them into the dark recesses like an Argentinian soccer player! Then this errant drunken jerkoff would proclaim, "These are the best wings EVER!" I could've fed him a deep fried rat that I had beaten to death in the parking lot covered in hot sauce!

Now, I wasn't the only person to perform this act of revenge! I started working in another place where one night, in a fit of rage, this bar maid is in the kitchen with me, extremely pissed off with having to cook a guy a hamburger at the end of her shift. More sports involving food ensued! I watched with glee as she turned the kitchen floor into a hockey ring and used this poor, defenseless meat patty as a puck, kicking it to score through such goals as: around the kitchen island, to the back door, and, somehow, almost inexplicably, up the back staircase! How much and what kind filth had this thing managed to amass?!? It was like some kind of bizarre bovine vacuum, sucking up lint, dirt, and an awful degree of assorted mouse shit! Then she proceeds to calmly cook this terrible fur burger, and says, "I'll probably just put some extra cheese on this to cover the damage!" I adored this girl! How could so much rage fit into such a tiny body?!? And, boy, did the floor sparkle! Apparently, animal fat works better than Mop and Glow!

Here was the really gross part. The owner would occasionally have these cookouts in the back pavilion on Sundays involving full chickens and ribs. He was really cheap, so any unused food would get unceremoniously thrown into the back walk in cooler. I WILL NOT waste food whatsoever, but here was the problem. The place was ill maintained, so the cooler would shut off occasionally, leading to a stifling environment, of perhaps some top secret government lab looking to grow some kind of new biohazardous germ warfare in petri dishes. This food would sit there for weeks! Now more sports activities would occur! We would be in a hurry to get cases of beer out of there to load the front coolers when we were busy, AND THESE FRIGGIN CHICKENS WOULD BE IN THE WAY! FOOTBALL, ANYONE?!? We would kick these things across the room like professional placekickers! THUMP! They would hit off the walls, off the cases of beer, and on a really spectacular day, depending on what kind of stilettoes or sandals we would be sporting, almost reaching the ceiling! Field goal for an extra point! Then, the unthinkable would happen. The owner would have another cookout, AND COMEPLETELY REUSE THESE THINGS! OH DEAR, GOD! HOW NO ONE EVER DIED THERE! Either it was the recooking in the barbecue pit, or the excessive alcohol consumption by the patrons that managed to kill all the salmonella in their systems, I'll never know!

Working at the same place, I met a fellow patron having the same abhorrence for something I did, though! Not only spiders, but SPOONS! I HATE spoons, and will absolutely eat nothing off of them! Soup, ice cream, whatever, I WILL NEVER, EVER, EAT OFF OF A GOD DAMNED SPOON! You might as well try chasing a vampire around with garlic! I tried to figure out what could have possibly happened to me in my life that would make me have such unbridled hatred for these things! The only idea that I could come up with, was that I was a finicky eater as a child and my parents would force feed me like a goose for foie gras!

A guy comes into the bar one day, and orders stew. So I bring him his meal with utensils. And then the screaming started! Normally, this would just piss me off, but he was shrieking that he couldn't eat with a spoon! Apparently he also shared my hatred of these utensils! I DON'T CARE! GIVE ME A FORK, A KNIFE, A SPATULA! JUST GET THIS SPOON AWAY FROM ME!!! Oh, thank God, to meet another person that was just as equally weird as me! (And that's really hard task to accomplish!)

Here is another weird story of my short bartending career at what I would like to refer to as my employment at Fern Hell. I am hired at this high class establishment to peddle wine at tables. Now, this was a terrible idea for two reasons. First of all, why the people who owned this place would think it would be an enterprising time during dinner to have me interrupt the joviality of their patrons enjoying their shitty food with me trying to sell my wares was beyond me! "Who would like to experience the wonders of, 'Upside Down Owl,' tonight?" Oh dear, God, I felt like such an asshole! I know the only kind I can afford! It comes in a box! Secondly, I have bartending experience, but it only involved asking blue collar workers if they wanted a shot or a beer! If I did serve wine, I would either ask white or red, and that's the extent of our selection here, folks! Screw merlot, shiraz, pinot grigio! ALL YOU EVER FUCKING GOT WAS EITHER WHITE OR RED! So, this was all very confusing to me! Occasionally, I would sell a bottle to some douche trying to impress his wife/girlfriend and/or family. He would smell the cork and then swish his glass around, take a sip, and proclaim, "The cork smells a bit nutty, but the after taste leaves a slight hint of a floral bouquet!"

So, now I go off to the local liquor store in the hopes of learning something! Oh, and I did, too! I try looking for these bottles in the high end section, much to no avail! Then I happened by the deadbeat, scrounger isle of the place, next to the Mad Dog and Manischewitz Concord Grape, where I found them! These idiots were selling these $8 bottles for $40 a pop TO EVEN BIGGER IDIOITS! And I WAS THE IDIOT TRYING TO SELL THESE THINGS! WHO WAS THE WORST GOD DAMN IDIOT HERE?!? (I don't even know, you decide!)

Then the mistress owner has the audacity to call me one day, to tell me I was fired! (Oh, don't threaten me with a good time!) "Maybe you would better off serving water here!" she exclaims! "MAYBE TAP WATER WOULD BE OF BETTER QUALITY THAN THE CRAP YOU HAVE ME WHORE OUT TO YOUR TABLES, INTERRUPTING YOUR CUSTOMERS' DINNERS, WHICH IN MY HUMBLE OPINION, HAVE NOTHING ON 'TUNA HELPER' OR A TWO DOLLAR JAR OF SPAGETTI SAUCE MIXED WITH ANGEL HAIR PASTA!" I scream back! (Which, coming and going from the kitchen all night, and witnessing the culinary horror, one would think it would TRULY be a step up from the low end junk that they would serve their customers!)

These same people who loved this garbage food, and would pay extraneous amounts for them, were the ones who would smell the corks! This lead me to instantaneously wonder why in my experiences, most rich people are so fucking stupid! This also brought along a long a myriad of unanswered questions in my mind! "What did these people do for a living to amass such a great amount of wealth? Maybe if they were originally born with it, and managed to salvage it, good for them! BUT WHY COULD NONE OF THESE NITWITS SEEM TO NOTICE THAT THEY WERE PAYING $10 for a glass of Rot Gut with a $40 plate of 'Chef Boyardee' or 'Ramen Noodles?" What was wrong with this elite clan?!? JESUS CHRIST!!! What was I doing wrong in life?!?

But I got my just revenge, though! A half a year later, this place ended up going under! What happened? Your new little wine bitch couldn't sell enough bottles to float your finances due to your shitty menu? What are you Cocknockers doing now?!? How's this working out for you all?!? Didn't see that train wreck coming, did ya's? Thanks for canning my ass, you did me a favor! Dicks!

This is another weird story involving me being a server. I used to work at this terrible restaurant downtown on the weekends aside from working at a quarry during the week. I thought this place sucked for a ton of reasons. First, and foremost, we were required to come to work 15 minutes early every day and do, "Chores." This would involve cutting up pies or bread or filling up bottles of ketchup, whatever. This wouldn't be so bad, but we weren't getting paid for it! We weren't allowed to punch in until our shifts started! How cheap does a restaurant have to be?!? They were only paying us $3.00 an hour! Was that extra time going to break the bank for these people?!? My time is just as valuable as yours! Secondly, they were even more cheap. Apparently, there was a gigantic tomato shortage that year! "Don't put any on any customer's salads, unless they specifically ask for them!" we were told! Who doesn't want a shitty iceburg salad at least without a fucking tomato?!? How much dressing could a server use to hide this missing factor?!? Thirdly, this place was just gross. The kitchen was missing half of its linoleum and the coolers were absolutely disgusting! How did this place manage to escape any inspections?!? (This is why I have completely stopped eating out! Your food MIGHT look great, but JESUS, I'd rather know what came from my own disgusting refrigerator!) Fourthly, all of our tips would be taxed at the end of the night! And then we would be required to split our tips with the hostess and the kitchen staff! Fifthly, we did not serve alcohol at this establishment, and that's how restaurants make money! And the higher the bill, the more the waiter or waitress makes! OH MY GOD! What was I doing, working for free?!?

I would go to the quarry every Monday and scream to the manager, "I hope that place burns to the fucking ground!" This went on for months, when suddenly one Monday, I come to work, and he tackles me! "Thank God you are OK!" he shrieks! "What the hell are talking about?!?" I scream back trying to breathe through his death grip! "Your diner just burned to the ground! Did you do it?!?" he says. "What the hell are you talking about? I just closed that place last night, and everything was fine!" I retort in confusion! Well, according to the news clips, apparently that did really happen! This greasy spoon was indeed crisped! Absolutely nothing was left! Oh, joy! Thank God!

Apparently, the bus boy managed to get into a fight with the cook, and lit the place on fire right after I closed up!

Go ambitious rage and undetectable mental disorders! This probably worked out to the owner's profit, because, due to the insurance money, he was able to build a much more viable facility! One that wasn't as disgusting as the former one! (Note to self: Hire insane people everywhere and always pay your insurance dues on time!)

# Other Weird Things Involving Tupperware Holding Food Probably of a Better Grade of What I Was Used to Serving

I don't know if this is just me, but does anyone else have this problem? I work a lot of hours doing construction, and would get up every morning to pack my lunch in the dark. Usually, it would just consist of trying to collect crappy leftovers or whatever I could find lurking in the fridge that wasn't rancid. Then, the unthinkable would happen! I would go to the four cabinets containing the Tupperware, AND NOT BE ABLE TO FIND ONE FUCKING LID OR BOWL THAT WOULD MATCH! NOTHING, ANYWHERE! How could I have four cabinets full of these things, AND NOTHING WOULD MATCH?!? And then the utter destruction would occur! I would open one of these cabinets, and an avalanche of unbridled plastic fury would hit me, and then the floor! "Mother Fucker!" I would exclaim, and much like the barmaid story earlier, I would start kicking this shit off of walls, the refrigerator, anything in general, depending on my enraged state!

The only things that would ever remain intact were Chinese takeout dishes. They are great in two respects! First of all, they will not ever disolve in your dishwasher, regardless of what heat setting you choose to use. Even if you use the, "Inferno" dial. Secondly, once you close these little buggers, they ABSOLUTELY WILL NOT open up in your vehicle no matter what your driving skills are! Are you on your side or upside down? Don't worry about being covered in yesterday's leftovers! They will not EVER open up under any unexpected circumstances! Who has the patent on these things?!? These ingenious, little bastards! (And I mean that as a compliment, too!)

# Other Things Involving Construction, But Not Involving Tupperware

If you have ever done construction, you work long hours, and try to amuse yourselves to make the time go by. Everyone would be obnoxious to try and get through the day. This one day I'm on this jobsite under a bridge, and this construction manager throws this five pound rock up in the air, and then another, AND THEN YET ANOTHER! NOW HE STARTS JUGGLING THESE THINGS! FOR A FULL MINUTE! I'm serious! He had these things going like a master magician! If he ever dropped one, someone would be spitting teeth out! I was mesmerized! Then he catches all these in midair and proclaims, "Well, now I have to go up to my truck, and get a shitload of paperwork done!" Wow, how both could one person be so irresponsible, but yet so responsible at one time?

Now, it was my turn to amuse the guys! Strangely, I had a set of police regulation handcuffs in my car. I know this sounds weird, but I never travel unprepared! I always have these and a gun under my seat! Most women travel with their lipstick or their collection of CD's entitled

"Rainforest Sounds," or some other assorted bullshit, BUT NOT ME, BABY! WHEN I ROLL, LOOK THE HELL OUT! I DON'T SCREW AROUND! So as a joke, I put one cuff on my left wrist and tell the manager that I had just escaped parole, and needed help. Well, I should have been more attuned to his lightning, stealth capabilities, because he suddenly grabs my other hand, too, and manages to lock that one up also! We were laughing so hard in the parking lot, until the unthinkable happened! Only the left one opened up with the key! The right one wouldn't open, AT ALL! It was completely stuck on my wrist! "Oh, My Fucking, God!" we both screamed!

He drags me under the bridge, where the laborers were working, holds my hand up in the air, and yells, "Can any of you people help this poor girl?" (At this point, I'm contemplating which is worse to happen to me on a jobsite, Aunt Dot unexpectedly visiting, OR BEING STUCK IN A PAIR OF CUFFS!) Then the quietest, middle age guy there on the scaffolding says, "Yes, I can do it." To which I reply, "This better not involve a Sawzall, because I don't know how good your aim is, AND THIS MY PROMINENT FUCKING HAND! I NEED THIS TO PLAY THE PIANO!" So now I get pulled back up above the bridge to the tool trucks. (Boy, it's so easy to drag a girl around in this capacity!) This guy gets out a can of WD-40, and hoses the lock down, inserts the key, and CLICK! It opens! Mesmerized with this man's plethora of skills involving both of carpentry and lock picking abilities, I ask him how he knew how to do that. He cryptically replies, "I think you ask too many questions." And then disappears off to continue working under the bridge once again. The weird thing was, no one there even questioned why I was stuck in a pair of handcuffs in the first place! I loved this crew!

# In Conclusion

Well, I think we've covered a lot of ground here concerning weird things, everything from involving turtles to tampons to spiders and spoons, which, in retrospect, in a literary aspect, both have a nice alliteration ring to them! Perhaps I should have entitled this book, "Turtles and Tampons," or "Spiders and Spoons," but I'm not sure what kind of audience that would have been attracted to it! (Who knows, though, maybe perhaps more, perhaps less! But I don't see it as a viable Christmas gift labeled in that capacity!) I figured the original title would be more suitable for most people. And as I have originally stated in the introduction, I hope this novella makes you feel better about your own shitty things that you have to deal with on a day to day basis. Just remember, never eat the bar food, just drink up! Enjoy!

........................................................................

OK, you know what? In post scriptum, here is one more weird story. When I was growing up, I had a very bad complexion. So I would wear tons of makeup to rival that of any Cosmopolitan or Vogue model in the hopes of people not noticing my true face! It was like a sheet rocker applying a five gallon bucket of spackle to a 4' X 8' wall every morning! (Don't get sad here, people, because this story turns out to be fucking hysterical!)

In 1996, the movie, "Barbwire" came out with Pamela Anderson. I thought she was the most beautiful woman imaginable! I am not a lesbian (and it's OK if you are one), but I wanted to look just LIKE HER! So I bleached my long, curly hair blonde, started tanning, and plucked out all my eyebrows. This in turn made me have to apply even more makeup around my eyes, but it was worth it, because I was so thin at the time, I achieved my goal! I was almost the spitting image of her! This was a really great idea, until the heat of summer rolled around! Then the drawing of the fake eyebrows became a completely daunting task! But that was OK, I would just let them grow back in! But here was the problem. They wouldn't! At all! Twenty years later, and I was still drawing them in! Great idea, Vaness! Millions of women are paying to have these things waxed, AND THERE WAS NOTHING I COULD DO, THAT WOULD GET THESE THINGS TO GROW BACK! I tried vitamins, massages, everything! ASOLUTELY NOTHING WOULD WORK WHATSOEVER!

I ended up working at this office where all the men were really laid back. So I tell this one guy the story out of general boredom one day, and he loves it! Then, SO IRONICALLY, the next day (and, I swear to God, this actually, really happened), the Project Manager comes in, and everyone does their morning routine of bitching about the jobsite. Then he says to me, "Hey, Vaness. My wife wants to get her eyebrows waxed, and asked me where to go. I thought yours were very pretty, so where do you go to have it done?" The other guy and I look at each other, and then proceed to fall off of our seats, under our desks, and almost die with laughter! "WHAT THE FUCK IS SO FUNNY AROUND HERE?!?" the Project Manager screams! The two of us are still rolling around giggling. Finally, the guy says, "Sir, she just doesn't have any!" "WHAT?!?" the Manager screams! "Here's my Cover Girl in Medium Bronze!" I squeal with laughter! "I really DON'T have any!"

This was particularly ironic, because this was an engineer who was in charge of inspecting the bridges that you drive upon every day, but yet could not notice fake eyebrows. Good luck with that structural inspection! He would probably, eventually end up courting a transvestite after his divorce for a few months, before realizing his terrible, erroneous mistake! (And, in my opinion, it's OK if you are one. I mean a transvestite, not a bridge engineer! One could probably give me some pointers on makeup and hair!) How unobservant some people are! It's mystifying!

Now, on a side note, concerning personal grooming, this pisses me off concerning makeup and men. How long does it take the average guy to get ready for work? Really? What, like, ten minutes? All you have to have to do is take a shower and have a cup of coffee. So let me tell you about a woman's regimen. First, this involves shaving pretty much every area on your body. Then the hair washing comes into play, followed by the extensive hair blow drying, depending on the length of it! (Boy, does this chew up a large amount of time! And don't forget if you have to dye it!) Now comes the makeup application part! But first, put your contacts in, women, because you might be able to depilatorize yourself without them like a blind bat using sonar, but this part would be absolutely impossible to master without them! (Nobody needs an eye poked out!) Innumerable amounts of cosmetics would then have to be administered (only rivaling the skills of a master trade contractor applying stucco!) involving such war paint as moisturizer, foundation, shiner, blush, eyeliner, assorted shades of eyeshadow, eyebrow pencil, mascara, and then lipstick! Tick Tock, Tick Tock! This is now followed by deodorant, hairspray, and then complete lotion application on your shaved legs to prevent dry skin from shaving! And don't forget to paint your toenails, ladies! Then you get to work, and instead of the guys complimenting you, they ask you why you look so tired! "MAYBE IF I DIDN'T HAVE TO GET UP TWO HOURS BEFORE THE REST OF YOU, I WOULDN'T LOOK SO SHITTY! SCREW ALL YOU MEN FOR YOUR LOW MAINTENANCE!" I always wanted to scream!

Anyway, this is the true, final end of my assorted collection (or collision) of weird stories! I hope that you enjoyed this little literary ride! I just hope that you buckled up first!

Printed in the United States
By Bookmasters